Debı

CHANGE YOUR M

"Here's a refreshing new take on changing your life. I found Debra's movie *motif* and examples to be a helpful way of learning to make positive life choices."

— Gay Hendricks, Ph.D. Author of *The Big Leap*

"Debra Oakland has written a book containing *7 Reel Concepts* that can and will change your life when applied. I found this book to be a refreshing way to compare our life's journey to that of a movie. As the writer, director, producer and star of our personal life movie, we take control of the desired outcome."

— Peggy McColl, New York Times Bestselling Author

Debra Oakland inspires us to imagine, create and step into courage to live the life we desire. Her innovative and entertaining writing style helps us to realize that we are the STAR of our own movie, therefore, we get write our own ending! Of course, I enjoy the terms of filmmaking because it's so close to me, but I have no hesitation recommending this read to anyone that is looking for a lift, courage or a way to step into the more fullfilling life they can see for themselves. Keep believing and refer to this book time and time again!

— Sandra Dee Robinson, Daytime actress, TV and Radio Host, Author, CEO and Founder of *Charisma on Camera Media Training Studio* and *Horsepowered Leadership Training*

"A courageous work of creativity that challenges you to be the STAR in your personal movie production, *Change Your Movie, Change Your Life* is a true hit! These 7 Reel Concepts for Courageous Change inspire the human spirit."

— David Riklan, Founder – SelfGrowth.com, the # 1 Self Improvement Site on the Internet

"We own 'our part' played in the film called 'My Life.' In this space, in our own personal editing room, we find freedom. Spend your life writing and rewriting, editing and scripting the life you dream about. You do it everyday anyway, now do it with awareness and attention. Debra Oakland's book will help you 'act vs react' to others and yourself. You will laugh, cry, hope and move forward to honor your past, present and future. If you live aware and you stay open to the edits, you will see your life is already an epic blockbuster major motion picture!"

— Wayne Scot Lukas, Celebrity fashion Stylist to the Stars | TV Show Host | His designs have been featured in the Metropolitan Museum of Art

"*Change Your Movie, Change Your Life* shows us the power of courage, healthy living, and taking personal responsibility for our lives, even in the face of difficulties. Debra Oakland shares practical and spiritual life wisdom with an authentic, empowered, and original voice. Bravo!"

— Melanie A. Greenberg, PhD, Writer of *The Mindful Self-Express blog* on *Psychology Today*

"From Debra's wise Heart and Mind to yours, take the actions she guides you through and your life will improve immediately and expansively. Turn to any page and you'll receive guidance to a healthier and happier life from someone who has had the courage to heal."

— Randall Fried, Writer | Director | Producer

"*I love this book!* Debra Oakland will teach you in these pages how to step out of your life, get a new perspective on any situation, and learn how to re-frame anxiety, worry or fear into gratitude, peace and positive action. Get it, read it, enjoy it, you're worth it!"

— Deb Scott, BA,CPC, Best-Selling Author | Award Winning Radio Host | The Best People We Know Show

"I applaud Debra Oakland's conviction of courage. *Change Your Movie, Change Your Life* is a testament to the 7 Concepts Debra has applied in her own life. I found this book profoundly deep, yet entertaining."

— Emmanuel Dagher, Spiritual Teacher | Author, Speaker & Kindred Friend

"Tap into YOUR creative potential and CHANGE the movie of your life! Progress with purpose and ON purpose! Debra Oakland eloquently reminds us to elevate our perspective and claim creative control of our lives! She inspires us to actively participate as the conscious producer and director of our personal life script so that our experiences reflect the creative genius of our soul. Beautifully written! A must read!"

— Cari L. Murphy, International Best Selling Author | Award Winning Media Host | Soul Success Coach

"*Change Your Movie, Change Your Life* provides 7 powerful concepts, presented in an entertaining way, yet deeply thought provoking. The movie treatments will touch your heart and stir your soul."

— Judy O'Beirn, International Bestselling Creator and Co-author of the *Unwavering Strength* Book Series

"Debra's book, *Change Your Movie, Change Your Life* connects you with the messages in movies and how they can powerfully impact your life. The 7 concepts explain how to compare your life's journey to that of a movie, where you get to be the producer, director and star! It is entertaining, enlightening and original, while giving you empowering ideas about manifesting your dreams."

— Nancy Mramor Kajuth, Ph.D, Author of *Get Reel: Produce Your Own Life*

"The cinematic metaphor may be a stroke of genius to some or a gimmick to others, but the message will trump all: Look within for the power to live an authentic life of abundance and gratitude. And get to the last scene of your life, proudly declaring, "Cut and print it!"

— Dr. Wendy Walsh, America's Relationship Expert | former Emmy nominated co-host of *The Doctors*

"Debra Oakland has been gracious enough to share her unique perspective on the spiritual path we all are traveling together, and *Change Your Movie, Change Your Life* will have you cheering as the final credits roll."

— Jack Armstrong, Intuitive Author of *Lessons from the Source: A Spiritual Guidebook for Navigating Life's Journey*

Debra Oakland is a beautiful example of living a life of courage and kindness. Having spent time with Debra in person and online, I have always found her to be a woman of integrity who is both creative and professional. Debra shows up for life with courage, kindness, grace, and love. Debra writes from her Heart and you'll feel her with you as you read her inspiring and fun book. I highly recommend you put *Change Your Movie, Change Your Life* on your must read list!

—Margaux Joy DeNador, Author of *The Art of Living a Life You Love* | Creative Life Coach | *Live Your Music* Radio Show Host

7 Reel Concepts
for Courageous Change

Change *your* Movie
Change *your* Life

7 Reel Concepts
for Courageous Change

Change *your* Movie
Change *your* Life

A LAGUNA INTERNATIONAL PRESS PRODUCTION

DEBRA OAKLAND

Published by Laguna International Press

www.LagunaInternationalPress.com

www.DebraOakland.com

Printed in the United States of America

First Printing, 2016

Cover Design by Paul Bond

Interior Design & Layout by Dudley & Margaux Joy DeNador

Disclaimer:

This book is designed to provide information and motivation to the reader. The movie treatments told within and their characters, names, places, events and incidents are either the products of the author's imagination or used in a fictitious manner. Any resemblance to actual persons, living or dead, or actual events is purely coincidental.

The content of each section is the sole expression and opinion of its author. Neither the author nor the publisher shall be liable or responsible for any physical, psychological, emotional, financial, or commercial damages, in cluding, but not limited to, special, incidental, consequential or other dam ages by the information or program contained herein. Our views and rights are the same: You are responsible for your own choices, actions, and results.

ISBN 978-0-9962150-9-1

Library of Congress Control Number: 2015914977

TABLE OF CONTENTS

DEDICATION

Change Your Movie, Change Your Life: 7 Reel Concepts for Courageous Change is dedicated to you, the reader, in the hope this book touches your Heart and stirs your Soul.

INTRODUCTION

"You have a voice, you have a choice. Apply both daily, and you will be on the road to personal freedom."

— Debra Oakland

HOW TO DIRECT YOUR OWN MOVIE AND LOVE YOUR LIFE

In the span of four years, I lost my 21-year old son, my unborn baby girl in my eighth month of pregnancy, both brothers and my father to prostate cancer a few years later. I also lost a number of dear friends during this time. Courage became a welcome companion. The outcome of what occurred over those few years could have turned out dramatically different had I not embraced the 7 Concepts in this book that helped me build a strong inner foundation of courage.

After the quick succession of loss, sadness, and grief, I asked myself what those who loved me would most want for me. I knew deep in my Heart the answer was to live a life of courage, choose to be happy, and encourage others. I had become a better person for having each of those who were in my life, if even for a short time; and I have become a stronger and more courageous person in their absence. I feel truly blessed for the time we had together. In my Heart, I love and honor each one as the precious gift they became in my life. My husband, Cody, and I have also applied these 7 Concepts in our marriage and have grown stronger and more resilient together.

The 7 Reel Concepts for Courageous Change I will introduce to you create a strong foundation of physical, mental, and spiritual support. I am confident these concepts will assist you in expertly directing the movie of your life. Aren't we all living in our own personal movie — written by, directed by, and starring ourselves? The goal is to direct your movie and love your life.

I look at life as my own personal, ever-changing movie reel. While some may question how I could be writing my own script when there was so much sadness in such a short period of time, I firmly believe we are where we are at any given moment in time based upon an infinite and sequential series of choices we have made in our journey. The seemingly random events that occur are our cues to speak, to act, or to react. Which direction the scene takes is not based on the events occurring in our lives but rather upon how we script our response. As the lead character in our mental movie, our feelings, our emotions, and our words are delivered while we direct our inner movie, sometimes with very little editing, but always in living color. When I think of my life as a movie, I realize I have the daily ability and opportunity to rewrite parts of my personal script or even compose an entirely new scene. Allow me to give you a look through the view-finder and show you how these 7 Reel Concepts reshaped my life and changed my movie.

Because I feel so much compassion for people going through loss and grief, I have become a Courage Advocate. The original definition of the word courage came into the English language from the old French word, corage, derived from the Latin word cor, meaning Heart — to tell the story of who you are with your whole Heart.

Here's my definition of courage:

I see courage as the will to act from the strength and Power within the Heart. Courage is a quality you gain through overcoming life's biggest challenges and something you become through experience. Living a courageous life happens when we allow the true essence of who we are to rise up and shine for the entire world to see — regardless of anyone's opinion of us. Courageous individuals who are true to themselves feel a powerful unshakable resolve, a true conviction of purpose and a willingness to carry on in the face of any challenge. Standing in the Power of purpose is a pure point of courage, available to everyone who cares to use it, which brings forward the Power alive within. If this Power has been diminished to the point of being dormant, when awakened it can shatter the fear of moving forward toward an intention or goal. Greatness arises from mediocrity. Lives are altered as awareness shifts to possibility and progress.

The union of courage and honor is a great gift within the Heart of every human Soul. My deepest desire is for us all to live courageously from the Heart. I cannot think of a better place from which to live. If you are having challenges being true to your potential and standing courageously when life seems out of control or too much to bear, take a moment for yourself. I offer my website as "A Spiritual Oasis — Encouragement for Overcoming Life's Biggest Challenges." Go to www.DebraOakland.com to sign up for my monthly "Living in Courage" newsletter. You will be courageously inspired. While you're there, download a complimentary copy of my e-book, *Living in Courage*.

Stepping out of comfort zones can feel daunting. I had written to an audience of one — myself — for most of my life. After Living in Courage was online, I began speaking and writing from my Heart with courageous conviction. After living through challenging times, I checked in with the theater of my awareness. The drama that had played out was soon over. Life had settled down, and I had some important choices to make. My ultimate goal was to become the conscious director of my personal life movie, rather than the reluctant supporting character. I knew in my Heart of courage writing was my dream. A long-repressed creative vision blossomed when I began writing this book, and I have found myself moving comfortably into the starring role.

MOVIE PREVIEW! TURN CELL PHONES OFF, PLEASE...

Before the curtains open, a little explanation is in order for you to get the most out of your viewing experience.

The first concept is Conscious Choice because it's your movie.

We move on to the Concepts on Wisdom, Love, Purity, Concentrated Illumination, Peace and finally Rhythm, which ties your entire personal movie-making skills together. It feels good to be the "conscious" writer, director, and producer of your own movie. The personal experience you gain by living through the trials and challenges in your life gives you a voice and a perspective you would not have had otherwise. It is wisdom. Unlike theory or book knowledge, wisdom can only be gained through experience.

Notice to Readers: For clarification, you will notice certain words are capitalized throughout the book. This is done on purpose, with purpose. It is my movie after all!

FOR YOUR VIEWING PLEASURE, EACH CONCEPT INCLUDES...

Debra's Storyboard — This is my personal spiritual health practice incorporating each concept.

Your Personal Storyboard — I have included a storyboard for you to fill out. I encourage you to take the time to do this right away. By doing so, you will gain personal insights into the concept that will spark your inner flame and help you integrate each concept more seamlessly into your daily walk.

A Movie Treatment & Rewrite of Movie Treatment — A treatment is an overview of the screenplay and is used to tell the story in a concise but compelling manner. For our purposes, we will use the treatment to give a real world illustration of the concept discussed in the chapter. The first treatment demonstrates how we live when we are not controlling the orientation of our energy. The treatment rewrite demonstrates how the same situation is handled when our energy is properly oriented, and we are living in our true Power.

Reel Wrap — Key personal movie-making moments that recap each concept.

Before The Curtain Closes...

Epilogue: Out Takes on Each of the 7 Reel Concepts — A short, condensed version of each of the concepts. This further illustrates the concept and helps you connect with what you have read, inspiring you to actively incorporate these 7 Reel Concepts to *Change Your Movie, Change Your Life.*

Reel Thoughts — It's a Wrap! — The afterword. This is my takeaway from writing the book. Trust me when I tell you the process of writing this book has been one of my greatest teachers. I often repeated the self-talk phrase, "Patience, Young Jedi." I made every effort to do so with a Heart of gratitude.

Nature Interlude: Through the Lens of the Camera — I have included a "short film" written by my dear friend, Steve Tallamy. This section is Steve's take on the 7 Reel Concepts with respect to our relationship with our environment and Mother Nature. Highly recommended!

Glossary of Terms — To help you understand any words or phrases with which you may not be familiar.

Finally, "**Roll the Credits**" acknowledges those who helped make this book possible.

WRITE YOUR OWN MOVIE FROM BEGINNING TO END

On the children's television program Sesame Street, the Muppets sang about life being like a movie, to write our own ending, to keep believing and keep pretending. Those Muppets made some good points! Write your own movie from beginning to end, never stop believing, and pretend all of your creations. By pretend I am referring to pre-planning your life. Think how children pretend when they are playing, using their imagination to create what they see as "reel" life by dreaming. They intuitively use their fertile imagination to creatively visualize their future. For adults I call this pre-tending; you can call it pre-imagining or anything resonating with your fertile imagination.

One of the reasons I chose movies as the core theme in this book is to present the Seven Reel Concepts to you in an entertaining way. It is my movie after all, and I do have some interesting Hollywood roots, but that's another story!

In each of our personal life movies, we have love scenes, birth, death, comedy, drama, roller coaster rides, car chases, wars, compassion, and a whole host of adventures featuring a cast of characters unique to each of us. These full, rich, immeasurably rewarding, and life-altering experiences shape and define who we become.

Any good movie maker knows challenges will cross their path, so it is good to use a variety of resources to overcome them. No one gets through this life without going through some challenges. How we choose to handle those challenges is what defines us. No obstacles, no growth. Embracing the life you consciously create liberates you. Your movie will never be a still life. The set design and cast of characters will change throughout your life creating a catalyst for transformation along the way.

No lead character in a movie production gets through without scuffs and bruises, at least not in any movie worth viewing. What would be the point? On any movie set, you have "the critics," as I call them. Criticism, judgment, gossip, blame, worry, anger and fear — oh, those pesky critics! Any star performer committing to these experiences of great contrast will find it requires tapping into their inner reserves of strength and courage. The twists and turns of the plot, much of which can reach epic proportions, require we draw upon these inner resources to reach those "Aha!" moments of understanding.

Mentally reviewing past episodes of the movie of your life assists you in understanding the purpose of many of the events from an elevated vantage point. It feels good to review as an observer, with resolution, and then release. We are all interconnected, sharing parallel circumstances, and can learn from the experiences of others. Our lives and ability to thrive and prosper depend on our right to say yes to our good.

Many aspects of ourselves are projected onto the screen of life.

There are scenes unfolding on our movie sets including a wide range of actors, supporting cast, locations, cameras, action and so much more. We take on roles to experience contrast, to grow and expand our spiritual awareness, learning what we want and do not want in life. This gives us the opportunity to write, rewrite, direct, film, and STAR in our own movie. Others are cast in supportive or non-supportive roles. Remember to check their resumes!

Your personal movie can be fun, exciting, joyful, abundant and full of love and support. Other times, it is a drama, filled with trauma, or it may even become a horror movie! The overwhelming majority of times we find ourselves in a frightening scene, it is usually a psychological thriller and not something physically threatening; however, should you ever find yourself in harm's way, you must respond courageously in a manner best protecting you and those for whom you are responsible. If we are able to detach from the projected "happy ever after" ending and live in the moment, we will make the right directorial decisions and find our movie much more enjoyable, right to the end. Being present NOW = Naturally Occurring Wonder!

So step back, and consider your own movie. Do you find yourself reacting or responding to people and situations? Are you portraying love or fear? What is your overall feeling as you watch the movie of your life? The best part is, if you don't like what you are viewing, rewrite the script and with authority shout out — TAKE TWO!

The information contained within these pages will assist you in different areas of life in support of your movie-making skills. Skillful movie-making requires attention to the intention of the film. Creativity, imagination, dedication, awareness, patience and a thousand other details are needed to polish the final version. If you are tired of experiencing the same predictable performances and want to change the movie of your life, you will have to do some rewriting and editing. This requires you take ownership and become the producer and director of your movie, as well as the leading star. By implementing the needed changes, your movie will progress with purpose on purpose.

There are fascinating people on our planet sharing their movies with us, giving a different perspective, which can open our Hearts to be and share more love. I am grateful to each of them for stepping up courageously and sharing their movie-making wisdom with the world.

I remain deeply respectful of the many varied belief systems people embrace throughout the world, most of which carry similar core messages of love, peace, integrity, service, grace and unity. Yet, the labels we place on people and things create comfort and, sometimes discomfort, in regard to beliefs. If this book makes you uncomfortable or disturbs your peace, think about remaining open to another way of thinking, feeling, and recreating the movie of your life.

If you are looking for ideas to assist you in the direction and production of your life movie, stick with me, kid — we are going places! I am here to support you by sharing some of the tools I use to bring more love, wisdom, and joy into my life. The 7 Reel Concepts in this book work for everyone, everywhere.

Concept #1:
CONSCIOUS CHOICE

Whose Movie is this Anyway?

"Take command, choose the outcome. Feel your passion of purpose; experience your role in full expression as you allow your purpose to permeate your being and world. As you do this, you are plugged into powerful energy that will pull resources, people, places — everything you need to you, in the perfect time and space."

— Debra Oakland

Imagine your life as an ongoing movie. What is the theme of your movie, and what "take away" do you want people to leave with? Keep in Mind we are all in this movie-making business together! In this giant theater we call life, the choices you make and the actions you take feature your own personal performance. We are all supporting actors in each other's films and the lead actor and star in our own.

Movies have a strong effect on us, because they trigger our emotions at a deep level. They take us out of our routine and allow us to experience a shift in perspective, showing us a more expanded version of what life can be. Movies put us in touch with our passion; they make us laugh and cry as our senses come alive with all manner of feelings pushing up to the surface. What do you do when a movie you love ends? You savor the way it made you feel as you put to memory your favorite moments in the film.

I am a sucker for independent films and short YouTube videos that inspire me. One of my favorite YouTube videos is *The Power of Words* by Andrea Gardner. Picture a blind man sitting on a busy street. Beside him is a tin can and a sign reading, "I'm blind. Please help."

A stylish young woman walks past him wearing a distinctive perfume. She stops, then comes back, and picks up his sign. She writes something on the opposite side, sets the revised sign down, and promptly walks off. Immediately, people begin dropping coins into the tin can as they walk past.

When the same woman comes walking back by the blind man, he asks her, "What did you do to my sign?"

She touches his shoulder and says, "I wrote the same thing but in different words."

The words she had written were: "It's a beautiful day, and I can't see it."

This short film demonstrates how the power of words and the resulting actions can transform a situation and create change. Your words carry power.

Do you ever feel like looking at life through a different lens? Ultimately the movie production, from beginning to end, is in your hands. Oops! Does it look like you are heading toward an unwanted surprise ending? There comes a time in our lives when we must decide what the outcome of our movie will be. Otherwise we may end up following someone else's vision for our life. Are you ready to rewrite your script or at least make a few alterations? It's only a decision away!

If you want to change your movie, you will need to make some changes in your life. Are you writing the script or allowing "the critics" (criticism, judgment, gossip, blame, worry, anger and fear) to inhabit the set of your film and to have creative license? Unless you have reached the status of film star, there are usually people on the set who will gladly tell you how your role "should" be played. They could be in wardrobe, makeup, lighting or even the caterer at the craft services table.

Please don't misunderstand me. I believe in showing respect to everyone on the set. An objective viewpoint at just the right time can sometimes be a lifesaver, and you must discern the quality and intent of the input. Sometimes you need to tell those critics not to "should" on your good!

YOUR PERSONAL PRODUCTION COMPANY

Your Power of conscious choice is activated by thought and leads to perception, understanding, logic, reason, courage, will, passion and enthusiasm. All these qualities are available and must be utilized in perfect synchronization toward the same goal and oriented toward the same purpose when we choose to live a life of positive purpose, productive impact, and meaningful permanence. We decide if the movie of our life is going to be a finely crafted masterpiece or a low budget zombie flick. The movie of our life is composed of countless scenes or short films strung together to eventually form the panoramic saga in which we presently reside. We are the result of these scenes, so it is important for us to see how the process begins. It all begins with the screenwriter.

The screenwriter receives a thought. At the moment of inception, we choose whether or not to acknowledge and accept the thought. This choice is made on the subconscious level and is usually the result of our personal programming. Our programming comes from our parents, peers, authority figures, environment and our own self-talk. It may be deeply ingrained from early childhood, but it is transformable. Once the choice is made to accept the thought, it is then perceived and evaluated. It is at this point the thought-form enters our consciousness and we, in our capacity as screenwriter, determine if the thought is logical and reasonable within the framework our programming has constructed. If the screenwriter decides the thought-form fits the construct of our perceived reality, it becomes the basis for our convictions, resulting decisions, and corresponding actions. From the initial thought, the screenwriter has gone through at least three decision points to create our script. The script contains the blueprint for the film we will use and the actions we will take to create a particular scene or a series of scenes for our movie. The script is then turned over to the producer.

The producer might be thought of as the Mind of the film project. The producer has the responsibility for underwriting the film and bringing together all the necessary elements to create the film of our life. Underwriting a motion picture in real life involves coming up with investors who are willing to put up the money to pay for the entire production, ensuring the film will be delivered on budget, and of the highest quality. In the movie of our life, it is the gathering of resources such as energy, time, and effort to make the movie happen. The producer rewards the screenwriter for creating the script and then decides which director, production designer, and director of photography to engage. We, of course, are the lead actor in our own film. It is critical for the success of the film that these roles are in synch and share the same vision.

The director has the responsibility to utilize the resources available to their best advantage in order to translate the script into the resulting film. The director is the creative passion and vision of the film; the director might best be thought of as the Heart of the film project. The director visually interprets the blueprint and guides the actors and performances. We know through experience our movie can be altered by one decision and, because we have free will, those choices are of utmost importance if we want to lead well-rounded, happy lives. The director is responsible for determining the outcomes that bring our movie to life.

It can be a challenge to take personal responsibility for our choices and decisions. It is always easier to believe life happens randomly or that we are victims of circumstance; but it isn't true. Adopting such an operational philosophy only leads to chaos, waste, and enslavement. Moving forward requires paying attention to even the smallest details and listening to the director. By making conscious choices supporting the varied areas in our lives, we begin to expand rather than contract. Tony Robbins says: "Using the power of decision gives you the capacity to get past any excuse to change any and every part of your life in an instant." Thought provoking, is it not? This is where the production designer comes in.

The production designer takes the script apart and breaks it down piece by piece. The overall genre of the film and the mood, appearance, location, lighting and angle of every shot in every scene is determined and planned out. This is another series of decisions sometimes made on a subconscious level but are more likely written out and visually represented before any film is shot. One of the basic tools of the production designer is the storyboard.

Once the production designer has planned out how the scenes are supposed to look, the director of photography has the job of recording the way we will eventually see the film. This includes decisions over which type of lens is used, which filters are employed, and at what angle the scene is shot in order to translate the recording of the director's vision onto the film.

Finally, there is the lead actor. After all of these countless decisions have been made, it all comes down to the director yelling, "Action!". Our cue to perform the scene. Nothing happens by chance. We determine the volume of our voice, the inflection and speed of our speech, our physical movements and gestures, and our facial expressions; all of it, an interpretation of the script, which started as a thought-form.

Let's look at an example. The thought-form of "healthy and physically fit" enters the screenwriter's awareness. The screenwriter decides this is a favorable outcome and produces a script featuring the lead actor eating healthy and exercising. The producer gives the screenwriter a warm and fuzzy feeling and sets about determining how to bring the script to life. A decision is made to hire a director who knows how to make action films; the production designer selects a gym and determines a daily workout regimen. The director of photography creates a storyboard of images showing you going from your present condition to a healthier and physically fit image of yourself, projecting it daily on the forefront of your consciousness.

The producer exercises conscious choice to provide a movie set where the craft services table only features healthy food, fresh fruit, and pure water, where smoking and excess use of drugs and alcohol are prohibited, and where exercise and sufficient rest are part of the daily schedule. This may mean rigorous exercise or might even require the star to engage a personal trainer, but a truly great film star will do whatever it takes to fulfill the demands of the role and bring the character to life.

The director exercises conscious choice to have the leading character rehearse saying the lines, "I think I'll have a salad."

The director will have the character repeat those lines until they flow effortlessly and sound natural. The director will have the lead actor (you) go through the action in the script repeatedly until your physical appearance matches the person first envisioned in the script.

Each scene of the movie of your life is the result of countless choices and decisions made based upon the orientation — positive or negative — of the production company of Mind.

RESPONSIBLE PRODUCERS ROCK!

One of the first steps in becoming a successful producer is to take full responsibility for everything created in and around your personal movie set. The blame game is over — become response-able. Blaming outside influences for how your life unfolds does not serve anyone and usually makes life unbearable for all involved. Wanting to change what is showing up in your movie, yet sitting back hoping your life will shift without doing something to make it happen, is a recipe for more of the same mediocrity and poor performance. Not a movie anyone wants to see!

What does the set design in your movie look like? Is it a happy, healthy environment where everyone works together, or are you allowing "the critics" to stand around and give their opinions about everything, creating doubt, and bringing down the happiness factor on the production? The choices we make each day design our life, because we write the script. The other voices, internal or external, have to be closely monitored and evaluated. True constructive criticism is always appreciated and helpful, but don't allow others to undermine or try to re-make your life according to their vision. Whenever you receive unsolicited advice, make sure to evaluate the perspective of the advisor and consider their motives.

This applies to you, too. We often turn the attention away from ourselves, because we are trying to fix our family and friends' movies. We get caught up in others' dramas and mistakenly think they so badly "need our advice." This is an easy way out for those eager to avoid dealing with their personal "stuff." As a critic, it's always easier to see what other people "should" do and much more challenging to step back and see ourselves in the same Light in which we see others. As a conscious, fully functioning human being, you can guide, but it is not your job to meddle in the life choices of another.

The best way forward is to focus your lens on living your own life in a responsible manner, making choices which support all life. Such choices include living and loving authentically, choosing peace, cooperating with the qualities of life expanding empowerment through the Heart, and having a grateful attitude and an open Mind. Stop and consider whom you most respect in your life. Is it the frantic friend who is regularly steeped in drama and ready to dish the latest gossip or is it the calm, cheerful friend who is confidently moving forward and never has a negative comment about anyone? You are who you choose to be.

Every movie goes through the editing process in order to get to the finished product. Not every scene shot makes it to the final film. Some scenes are best left on the cutting room floor of Apology, because they don't add anything positive to the production. The acting was overly dramatic. The lines were not delivered with the right intention or inflection. The actress may have made less than desirable choices on how to play the scene, causing confusion or misunderstanding. Just because you did the scene does not mean you have to hold on to the scene and carry it with you for the rest of your life. Learn to forgive and let it go.

The best editing tool available is the power of conscious choice. Every moment gives you a perfectly new opportunity to focus your efforts on living your best life and leaving the less than stellar scenes behind in the dust bin of Forgotten. You have the power to rewrite a script that doesn't work. You can even make the choice to throw out a script and start over from a different perspective. Your goal is to keep only those scenes showing you in the best light and reveal the brilliance of the character you were meant to be, that's a movie people will clamor to see! It all begins with you. How will you project your vision out in the world? I always say, "Responsible Producers Rock."

DIRECTORIAL DECISION TIME

It's decision time, folks! As writer, director, producer and editor of your thoughts, feelings, and actions, your directorial decision to consciously or unconsciously create will determine the outcome of your movie. You make a difference in people's lives as they interact in your energy field, noting the living example of excellence you present as the director of your daily life. This is much better than trying to force someone to see things your way.

It is not your calling to determine how they will choose to perform their supporting role in your movie; however, as the director of your own film, it is your call as to whether or not they remain as a member of the cast. You do not know the path others' lives can or must take in this lifetime. Their past, present, and future choices will determine what shows up for them, just as your past, present, and future choices will determine how much joy or suffering will show up on the living screen of your life. You must be open to the possibility there may come a time when you have to let someone in a supporting role go if their performance is undermining the quality of your life.

If you want change, you need to be the captain at the helm of your own ship, like Cap'n Jack Sparrow on the Black Pearl in the movie *Pirates of the Caribbean*. You are sailing into the unknown to create your own adventure. Being first mate will not guarantee the results you are looking for. Someone else dictating the possible outcome does not put you in the captain's seat. When you find yourself cast in a supporting role, make sure you are responsible for your choices.

CHOOSE YOUR SUPPORTING CAST

Thomas Mitchell was one of America's great character actors and appeared in more than a hundred films and television productions. *Gone with the Wind* would not have been the same without his portrayal of Scarlett's father, the indomitable Gerald O'Hara, or Hattie McDaniel's moral counterpoint as Mamie. Sometimes it is the supporting actor who serves as the catalyst for the great dramatic turnaround. The lead character, Scarlett O'Hara, realizes she had been behaving in a selfish and irresponsible manner. She is eventually forced to accept the reality she created for herself instead of the fantasy of a life now gone with the wind.

Being a character actor in a supporting role can be a rewarding experience filled with the richness and color of life. It all boils down to the choices you make about how you play the part.

Our world is one of duality and contrast. Light-dark, up-down, forward-backward are continual opposites we all view and experience differently. For some, this world is a pristine place of beauty and abundance filling their lives with joy and peace. At the opposite end of the spectrum, other people see the world as disappointing and fearful, a place where they have to struggle to get ahead. Constantly blaming others or outside circumstances for the progress of your movie brings even more negative critics to the set, reflecting right onto the movie screen of your life. Love and appreciation will transform any movie set, bringing positive elements into every scene.

Where you choose to be (your vantage point), and for how long, will determine your view. You can make changes from wherever you are in life — it's never too late. An old dog can learn new tricks. Can you think of a better time and place to start than now? All it takes is conscious choice. When humanity wakes up to the fact we are all interconnected, this world will shift dramatically. By concentrating on creating and directing the best movie of our life, we help shift the bigger moving picture, making us part of the solution.

CREATIVITY = DIRECTING ENERGY

All life is energy in motion. Thoughts, feelings, and intentions are energetic frequencies carrying us into the experiences of our life's living motion picture. One of our greatest opportunities is learning to direct this energy. Cause and effect determine how things manifest outwardly in our lives and are a direct result of how we manage our energy. Cause is our focused thought or the recurring habits of our thinking, feeling, and actions, which create effects or outcomes in our lives. Being creative contributes to our happiness and vitality. Think about how you feel when you are in creative mode. It feels exhilarating. When people feel as if they have nothing to create, nothing to contribute, unhappiness begins to permeate the Body, Mind, and Spirit.

Children endlessly create. Their movies are fascinating to watch! They are constantly reminding us to reconnect with the magical energy we may have let go of as adults. Children are full of energy, running about, looking for more joy as they happily use the power of their imagination. Albert Einstein said: "Creativity is contagious, pass it on." As any parent will tell you, children are full of wonder, enthusiasm, and determination as they express their creativity.

BODY, MIND, AND SPIRIT — THE TRIAD OF YOU

When you focus on and are grateful for what you presently have, instead of worrying about what you don't have or what you want, positive shift becomes a natural occurrence. Healthy, happy, and constructive creative thoughts affect all areas of our lives in a positive way; whereas worrisome, fearful thoughts affect our lives in a negative way. Whether we vibrate to positive or negative energy, it's important to know one or more parts of our whole being are likely to be affected. It is simple physics.

Human beings are triune entities — the triad of you. We comprise three separate components making up the whole. These are commonly referred to as BODY, MIND, and SPIRIT. The Body is the protective suit in which we navigate the human experience. It is the representation of who we are and the image people recall when asked if they know us, but it is not, in any way, the complete representation of who we truly are.

In order for us to operate with maximum efficiency and productivity, we must properly maintain our body and well-being. No matter how attractive and alluring we make this physical housing, it must never become the focus of our identity, because it is finite and transitory. Our bodies age and begin to show the wear of our lifestyle choices. Even the most beautiful, physically perfect human body eventually ages and deteriorates. It is a vessel housing the other elements of your being: a temple within which dwells your true divinity.

Between the physical body, which is temporal, and the Spirit, which is our true and eternal essence, lies the battleground of the human experience. I call it Mind. It is the part of us every religion, philosophy, curriculum, and ideology tries to define, develop, and direct. It is similar to your physical brain in that it is composed of two aspects operating in a similar manner but usually from completely different motivations, much like the memory and processor of a computer. In this case, the two parts combine to establish the orientation of our intention.

The first part is what we commonly call the Head which perceives and analyzes stimulation in a predominantly analytical manner in order to determine a proper response. It is the mental counterpart of our physical brain and is the Source of our thoughts and ideas. Its primary objective is to provide our perception with a framework or structure of logic and reason upon which to reference and project our life experience.

The second part of Mind is the Heart, which responds to stimulation in an emotional and often undisciplined manner, providing us with motivation. If the orientation of our intention is positive — moving from Source through us into the world — our motivation is to react in a constructive manner. We are functioning as a conduit for and manifestation of a positive and constructive Power.

If the orientation of our intention is from physical stimulation inward, there is often confusion, strife, guilt, anger, hatred, and various other manifestations of negative energy with unstable frequencies. Mind becomes oriented toward self and every perception or response is biased toward a false perception of who we are.

The flow of energy is slowed, and the Power becomes negative.

At the core of your being is Spirit. It is eternal, because it is pure energy. It is enlightened, because it is pure Light. It is enriched because it is pure Love. It has no sex, race, creed, or ethnicity because it is part of the One. Spirit is the part of us created in the image and likeness of the Divine, the Source, and the Universe; which many refer to as God. Spirit's purpose is to bring Light and Love from Source into the physical world via Mind.

One of the immutable Laws of the Universe teaches us energy is active and dynamic. It flows toward that which creates potential. If it flows in the proper direction, energy runs machines, empowers computers, and lights the world. When energy flows in the wrong direction, it can be destructive. When both aspects of Mind, the Head and the Heart, function in synch, they produce phenomenal Power. This Power can be constructive or destructive based upon the direction of the energy flow; the orientation of our intention. If the Head and Heart are out of synch and oriented in opposite directions, the result is indecision, confusion, and chaos.

We are here to live a life motivated by perfect Love and illuminated by perfect Light in order to bring the Peace and Love of Source into the human existence. There are many who believe we will come back in a different physical package and repeat this process we call living until we achieve perfect flow, harmony and Oneness. Others believe we only get one shot at it and then face evaluation and eternal reward. The details may vary from tribe to tribe, culture to culture, tradition to tradition, dogma to dogma; but the parts and the goals are predominantly the same when you strip away the various subjective interpretations of the objective infinite.

> *"The moment one definitely commits oneself, then Providence moves too. All sorts of things occur to help one that would never otherwise have occurred... unforeseen incidents, meetings, and material assistance, which no man could have dreamed would have come his way."*
>
> — William H. Murray

OUR MENTAL MOVIE STUDIO

For anything to manifest in physical form before your eyes, there needs to be a thought-form, which sparks a vision, and a dream manifesting a desire. Just as the great movie director/producer Stephen Spielberg weaves his plots to arrive at a predetermined climax, the extent to which he begins with the end in Mind is a powerful determinant of his creation. We all have a favorite Spielberg film or films that have touched us deeply on some level.

Let's say you want to build a movie set, and on this set you need a tree house for several scenes. First, you make a mental blueprint in your Mind of the details, next a blueprint to follow on paper before you choose the materials or hammer the first nail, which leads to the physical creation. This also helps you determine the cost of this piece of scenery and decide whether it is within your budget. Before you built this beautiful tree house, you envisioned it in its full completion, felt the joy of it being built, and became motivated to take the appropriate steps, knowing it would be the perfect prop in your movie.

Everything we see with our eyes or engage with our senses is a creation brought forth in someone's Mind. This thought was nurtured and birthed through energetic vibration. Our passion and attention to the art and science of the act of "creation" bring it into reality more quickly and determine its duration. Our thoughts are a powerful engine creating the reciprocal force of our feelings, in combination with the determination of our will, to propel our creation forward or backward.

Within the collective "I" of each of us lies the answers we seek. In the production company of Mind, decide to use your role as casting director to find people who are willing to play strong supporting roles in your movie. Many will show up to audition. Not all will make the cut simply because they don't fit the theme of your movie. Learn to let go, and don't try to force someone to be something they are not. Some characters will stay as long as both of you find value in each other, and then they will move on when the important role they played in your movie has ended. Learn to appreciate the significance of another's contribution, no matter how small it may first appear to be. A course correction of one degree is only truly appreciated after many miles. One small comment made in a moment of poignant honesty can dramatically alter the course of one's life, changing tragedy to triumph.

It is also important for you to provide strong character support in the movies you audition for. Don't forget your participation in their movie is just as important as theirs is in yours. When filming a movie, one scene at a time is set up and carefully reviewed before the cameras begin rolling. It does not unfold all at once. If every door opened at once, what would be the purpose of the journey, of learning contrast, of experiencing all aspects of ourselves?

Think of life as the greatest movie ever made! One scene at a time, the story of our lives ever unfolding, opening doors we predetermined arriving at along the way. What a perfect way to expand our Souls experience as individualized aspects of God/Goddess. Brilliantly simple, yet we endlessly complicate it. When Love becomes the ultimate goal, we have a worthy purpose and a desired destination. The journey is where growth, self-awareness, and expansion happen. We made a conscious choice in the highest state of awareness, as individual creator beings, to place ourselves in physical forms in order to test the waters of contrast and free will, as did billions of others. Dan Rather said it well, "If all difficulties were known at the outset of a long journey, most of us would never start out at all." I quite agree with him. This "experience of life" can be a long and sometimes arduous one. Had I known the time and work that would go into this book, I might well have never begun. I trusted my Heart to move forward and am most grateful I did.

OUR CHOICES & DECISIONS = OUTCOMES

The choices and decisions we make and how we choose to handle our experiences defines the story line in our movie and the outcome. Decision time. Hmmm, here is some contrast; will I choose love or fear?

Dorothy in *The Wizard of Oz* maneuvered through every challenge confronting her on her journey down the Yellow Brick Road, navigating all manner of contrast before coming to the realization running away was not the answer. There truly is no place like home. Think of home as a return to Source, to Love. Our decisions determine the course of our lives.

As eternal beings traveling the expanse of the Universe, it will become clear what is most important is our bliss. Joy-full being-ness. When you show up each day for the roles you will play on the screen of life, be sure to bring a joy-filled Heart to the set. Radiating your Light sets you up as the director and lead actor who is willing to set an example for your cast of characters. Living fully engaged in the present moment builds momentum as rich awareness expands in the many areas of your life, keeping you in the flow and in the know. It is also one of the most challenging activities to master in a world filled with distraction.

Change is constant, so if you notice new things with fresh eyes, this keeps you present and engaged in the moment. Without judgment, become the witness, the observer, and engage your senses. The wise and revered Joseph Campbell told us, "Follow your bliss and don't be afraid, and doors will open where you didn't know they were going to be." How exciting it is to follow the path of your own inner bliss.

The Alchemist, by Paulo Coelho tells the story of a young shepherd named Santiago, who is able to find a treasure beyond his wildest dreams. Along the way, he learns to listen to his Heart and, more importantly, realizes his dreams, or his Personal Legend, are not just his but part of the Soul of the Universe.

Separation from each other separates us from the grace of Oneness. When Oneness is embraced, we will live in unity, peace, and a state of loving compassion. The overall lesson I took away from The Alchemist is that we are all part of the Soul of the Universe. We are spiritual beings, living individual lives of duality, who will one day return home to the Heart of Love and Light so much wiser and more fulfilled from our experiences.

CHOOSE TO BE PRESENT FOR YOUR MAGICAL MOVIE MYSTERY TOUR

Nothing is accomplished without action. Thought = feeling = action. All are important parts of action, beginning with thought, which has been a highly underrated action step involving much confusion. Start to question and investigate why the tremendous Power of thought has been repressed. Reclaim your Power by stepping out of the shadows of fear and doubt. By choosing wisely and taking the necessary steps to make your dreams happen, victory is yours to claim.

Without our bodies, we are spirit beings; pure energy forms created out of the thought-form of the Universe. What is thought? Many believe thought is the response to external stimuli. The part of our being known as Mind — which comprises our Heart, our intellect, and our emotion and reasoning — responds to stimuli coming into us and flowing through us either from the external, physical world or from our internal, spiritual Source. Stimulation creates a response. The response takes the form of a concept and a thought is formed. It may show up as a picture, a word, or an emotion; but, whatever form it takes, our Mind tries to immediately categorize it and make sense of it in our conscious awareness. The Laws of the Universe, pure physics, dictate that stimulus creates response. For every action, there is an opposite and equal reaction; positive and negative, Light and dark, masculine and feminine, Yin and yang; Dharma and Karma. Thought interpreted into feeling and giving birth to action.

No one else can think for you. You have a voice, and you have a choice, which puts you on the road to personal freedom. Yes, people can encourage you to change your thought, but the thinking is up to you. Think of your inner Power as regenerative, a deliberate creation at its best. This is more than self-improvement. It is self-alignment: reorienting our self to produce a positive and powerful alignment of our Mind, which brings us back to center, back to balance, and puts us in control of our lives. There is immense Power in being in charge of all your thoughts. Together, with our combined thoughts, feelings, and actions, we can and will change the world.

The goal is achieving equilibrium; where the flow of energy from the outside physical world is balanced by the flow of energy from our spiritual Source. When the external, physical influence is highly negative and toxic, we have it within our being to choose how we are going to respond based upon our internal orientation. If our orientation, our focus, our warrant has been given from the physical environment inward, Mind will respond accordingly even to the point of self-destruction. If we choose to orient ourselves to Source, our reception of and attunement to the spiritual stimuli is greater than of the physical, and our intentions determine our responses, which result in actions producing a more desirable outcome.

Shift happens in our life when we disengage from discord and the old triggers of our negative nature and, instead, engage the infinite Power of Love as the foundational root of our response and thought creation. Embracing the "Power of Conscious Choice" reminds us we get to decide what happens in our life. Whether we are in a good place or a bad place, we are where we are at any given time, because of a series of decisions we made sometime previously in our lives. Becoming aware of this fact is the beginning of creating the life we were meant to live and impacting the world around us in a positive and healing manner.

If you don't like where you are, make different choices. Take back control of your life. Become aware of the thoughts you create and the choices they engender. Your life will change when you decide to radiate the many qualities of Love out into the world. To radiate these qualities, you must first access them for yourself. You do this by daily making the decision to orient your intention to Source. Consciously choose to orient toward Spirit and allow yourself to be a channel for transmission of the Divine Will in your life. This will illuminate your thought process and enlighten your emotional responses.

When someone cuts you off in traffic, your first response may be that the driver is in a hurry to get somewhere and is distracted, perhaps dealing with drama or even tragedy. What if this person is put in your path for a purpose? Instead of flipping them the bird, you send them a blessing thought. Your whole environment will change, because it will be influenced by the best qualities within you; qualities derived from and enhanced by Light and Love. What a way to supercharge your day and theirs!

LITTLE OL' AWARENESS EXPANDER YOU

How about becoming an awareness expander? Use your imagination as you did as a child. This is a Power that is eventually hidden from us by the bombardment of stimuli from the outer world, which makes it easier to become "critics" in each other's movies and submit to a minor role in the collective movie being run by those who truly understand the Power of thought.

Here is a simple exercise you can do right now to begin to reclaim your Power. Say to yourself,

> *"I choose each day to be the conscious director of my own movie. I always retain my inner Power and vision for the outcome I choose to experience."*

By taking hold of your mental and feeling worlds, you become a master movie maker. Who better to do it than you? Expect to yield the optimum results you want on the Soul explorations you choose to experience. The final choice to externalize anything is up to you.

The decision to be present moment to moment aligns us with NOW — our Naturally Occurring Wonder. As we become more skilled at living in the present moment with our attention on our Perfected Presence, what happens? Awareness takes hold, and clues, messages, intuition and wisdom become way-showers. No longer controlled by the distractions of the outer world, we find ourselves becoming fully connected to our inner Power — Heart directed and Light directed; fearless, peaceful and joyful for all the abundance life has to offer.

Everything is affected by our functioning in the world as a fully expanded being of Love and Light. We carry a deep responsibility to express gratitude for this gift of life. We are so much more than these physical forms, yet they are to be loved, respected, and appreciated in all their glory. Enjoy life, savor it, knowing one day you will be amazed at the magical mystery movie tour you individually guided, directed, produced and starred in. As we begin new Soul explorations, it will become clear the Power was always within, and we never had to go without.

MOVING PAST LIMITATION

How content would you be if you were living a non-creative life? Creating is what we are here to do. Sharing our creations with others brings us fulfillment and happiness. Just think back to how great you felt the last time you accomplished something or created something. Maybe it was when you were a child, but you need to reclaim that feeling. Savor it. Wrap yourself in it and embrace it. Choose to make the attainment of feelings of accomplishment the focal point of your life's mission. When one accomplishment is completed, anticipate how good it is going to feel to achieve another creative endeavor. What great movie producer or director stops at one movie? As we make a conscious choice "to do" a thing, we feel fired up and excited. We learn to begin with the end in Mind.

Like any successful director, learn to focus like a laser beam on the one thing you desire to accomplish in your movie. This lowers the idea into your consciousness until you can see it, feel it, smell it and taste it. Our senses are there to support and guide us. Learning to use and trust them creates an open door to our success. To expand mentally, physically, and spiritually, it is important our creations are a blessing in and to all life. This is where we benefit from developing the proper Soul orientation and self-control. It allows us to keep in Mind harmlessness is always a good objective.

Rejecting negative outer influences you have carried around most of your life is like a breath of fresh air. As a filmmaker using single minded focus, imagination, and determination, you will be able to star in and produce the most amazing movie you can dream up. Be willing to do whatever it takes to succeed in all you wish to accomplish, never giving up, because you deserve to live in the movie of your dreams. Take full responsibility for your life, and your life will reward you with even greater accomplishments.

Preceding any accomplishment there comes the desire and the decision "to do." Engaging the Mind and Heart in all we wish to experience brings harmonious, balanced activity into the film we desire to develop, helping to release limitation. Once one creative accomplishment is under our belt, it is easier to move on to another and another. Before long, you will be eager to pay it forward by sharing your film about "The Power of Conscious Choice" with those who notice your enthusiastic attitude in all you do.

There is magnetic Power in conscious choice connecting us to our Heart, which loves to bring us what we desire. By moving past limitation and being courageously inspired by an unlimited attitude and feelings, what we decide to be will be! Our world is a creation. We are here to create our own worlds, within the world, many smaller movies within the bigger moving picture of life. The proof of human accomplishment is visible everywhere. Whatever the Heart believes, the Mind conceives.

None of us view the world in exactly the same way, yet we all create in unique ways of value that can be shared with others. If we all sang the same note, there would be no music; if we only knew one word, there would be no language; if there were only one color in nature, it would be devoid of contrast. If one can do it, anyone can. You and I were given the ability and the responsibility to tap into our greatness, to define our individuality and unique gift of the Soul.

In *Dead Poets Society*, Mr. Keating (played by Robin Williams) tells his students:

> *"Carpe diem. Seize the day, boys. Make your lives extraordinary."*

Since we are making choices that create in every moment, why not consciously direct these creations in a positive direction? For those who are caught up in negativity, there are many people happily waiting on the positive side of creation to assist you!

There are two choices, love and fear. The Power of conscious choice sets you free. The love, wisdom, and Power in our Hearts will serve as a perfect guidance system. The best part is it is freely available for all who choose to use it!

DEBRA'S STORYBOARD ON CONSCIOUS CHOICE

I will be sharing with you my daily spiritual movie-making practices for each of the 7 Reel Concepts throughout the book. Here is the first...

I found meditation difficult in the beginning. I was trying to do it in ways I had read or heard about growing up. Each person needs to find the form of contemplation best suiting their life. For example: sitting in a garden, reading, singing, walking, meditation or prayer, swimming in the ocean, enjoying time with anyone or anything you love. There is no right or wrong way to connect to our Source. Our connection to the God of our knowing is sacred, as individual as we are, and deserves our deepest respect.

Gratitude is foremost in my Mind when waking in the morning and before sleep. The day begins and ends in appreciation for all that is here and all on its way into my life. Sitting quietly in the morning when the house is quiet is the best meditation time for me, when my Mind is still between sleep and waking. To spend quality time each morning and evening connected to my inner Source of love, wisdom, and Power has steered me through life, guiding me in miraculous ways. The outcome of my movie matters to me.

Silent awareness gives me the opportunity to listen to the voice of my Higher Self in sacred space. Life is busy and getting busier with the new technologies allowing us to connect with people around the world. The irony is the more platforms technology brings us to communicate, the less we speak with each other; the less we truly communicate. It is more important than ever to be still and listen to the all-important quiet, resonant voice within. I ask questions, make decisions, contemplate, allow and deal with whatever needs attention.

Eternally grateful I AM for this sacred space within myself I connect with daily. Gratitude is always at the top of my list! A great way to begin and end each day is to write down or give thanks for seven things you are grateful for. Seven is a spiritually significant number. By the time you have begun writing the seventh manifestation of gratitude in your life, you will notice your awareness has shifted, has expanded and reoriented, from the noise to the joys.

YOUR PERSONAL STORYBOARD ON CONSCIOUS CHOICE

Do you find yourself in need of some encouragement to make better choices? This is a tool I use to help me focus on what is important. I call it my storyboard. A storyboard is a graphic organizer used in movie-making for the purpose of visualizing a script before any scenes are shot. Where the script is a written "plan" for the film, the storyboard is the first visualization of the film. It is put together by the production designer to help illustrate the visual style of the film and plan the shots.

For our purposes, we write down our goals and dreams, our personal movie script. By adding the kinetic aspect of filling out the storyboard, we apply another one of our senses to reinforce the process of bringing our reality in alignment with our vision. I use this tool to sharpen my focus on the various aspects of my daily spiritual ritual. A personal storyboard is included for you at the end of each concept, and I invite you to incorporate this tool in your visioning process. I often think of this quote by an unknown author: "Hold the vision, trust the process."

YOUR PERSONAL STORYBOARD ON CONSCIOUS CHOICE

1. Upon awakening in the morning, I consciously and purposely choose:

____

____

____

____

____

____

2. Before starting my day, I choose to take a moment for my personal spiritual ritual by:

____

____

____

____

____

____

3. Choosing to align Mind with Spirit, I recognize my unique talent or gift as:

____

____

____

____

____

____

4. In my daily work, I choose to represent gratitude by:

____

____

____

____

____

____

5 When someone hits one of my "tripwires," I now consciously choose to:

____

____

____

____

____

6. In Light and Love, I make the Conscious Choice to make different choices regarding:

____

____

____

____

____

7. Before going to sleep at night, I set these Conscious Choice intentions:

____

____

____

____

____

#1 — TREATMENT FOR SCRIPT ON CONSCIOUS CHOICE

FADE IN

My husband, Cody, answers a call from the hospital at five o'clock on a Sunday morning. It is news a mother never expects to hear. There has been a car accident. My son has died.

First: disbelief. This can't be happening! You never expect to lose a child before your own life is complete. Please God, make this go away. Shock sets in; indescribable pain permeates my entire being. I had been through so much loss already. Now I have lost my only child and am heartbroken....

In a state of shock, feeling disconnected and out of body, I have to decide how to begin handling this news. Family is calling; people are trying to connect out of concern and love.

I want to sit and be still. No, that doesn't feel good. I need to get up and move around, go somewhere. No! That doesn't work either. What to do, where to turn, how to function? Cody is my rock, but he is in shock as well. How do we get through this loss? How do I comfort us both? I can't. Not now!

Depression sets in, unable to function on any level; the days drag on to become weeks, months, and years. Life has lost its luster. There seems to be no hope of feeling normal again. Tears flow endlessly, guilt, self-pity, and hopelessness become close friends. My marriage is lifeless, and I see no hope of it changing. My greatest fear is to be hurt again by loving so deeply.

Cody can no longer live in this sad and broken marriage. As he takes his leave, he is wishing it would have all turned out differently. It could have all turned out so differently.

FADE TO BLACK

#1 — REWRITE OF TREATMENT FOR SCRIPT ON CONSCIOUS CHOICE

FADE IN

My husband, Cody, answers a call from the hospital at five o'clock on a Sunday morning. It is news a mother never expects to hear. There has been a car accident. My son has died.

First: disbelief. This can't be happening! You never expect to lose a child before your own life is complete. Please God, make this go away. Shock sets in; indescribable pain permeates my entire being. I had been through so much loss already. Now I have just lost my only child and am heartbroken....

In a state of shock, feeling disconnected and out of body, I have to decide how to begin handling this news. Family is calling; people are trying to connect out of concern and love.

I want to sit and be still. No, that doesn't feel good. I need to get up and move around, go somewhere. No! That doesn't work either. What to do, where to turn, how to function? Cody is my rock, but he is in shock as well. How do we get through this? I make a conscious choice to find a way out of this despair. I must believe Love is greater than even this situation.

Cody and I decide to comfort each other as we talk about how to get through this loss. I ask myself an important question, "What would my son, who loves me as I love him, want most for me?" I say to my husband, "Knowing the love we all carry for each other is on a deep Soul level, the only answer is that he would want us to live a happy life, celebrating his life as a gift, grateful for the time we had together."

I choose to define my life by handling this loss with courage, strength, and peace. My marriage to Cody grows stronger, and we become more resilient together. I realize there are different ways of responding to hardships and that we can change our perspective from within. Both Cody and I rely on a strong foundation of inner Power that houses our courage and strength, knowing this is the way to celebrate and honor my son's life. We carry him in our Hearts as a precious gift. I embrace life with peace, gratitude, and compassion. I find the silver lining by going into the world courageously and helping others through the process of loss and grief.

FADE TO LIGHT

REEL WRAP: THE CONCEPT OF CONSCIOUS CHOICE

★ Imagine your life as an ongoing movie. You are the screenwriter, producer, director and lead actor in your own film and have supporting roles in others' films.

★ Are you writing the script, or allowing "the critics" (criticism, judgment, gossip, blame, worry, anger, and fear) to tell you how it "should" be written?

★ Your programming comes from your parents, peers, authority figures, environment and your own self-talk. It may be deeply ingrained from early childhood, but it can be changed.

★ The blame game is over. Become response-able. Blaming outside influences for the way your life unfolds does not serve anyone and usually makes life unbearable for all involved.

★ One small comment made in a moment of poignant honesty can dramatically alter the course of one's life, changing tragedy to triumph. Learn to let go, and don't try to force someone to be something they are not.

★ When both aspects of Mind, the Head and the Heart, function in synch, they produce phenomenal Power.

★ Whether you are in a good place or a bad place, where you are at any given time is based on a series of choices you made sometime previously in your life.

Concept #2: WISDOM

What's in the Fortune Cookie?

"True wisdom is a personal conviction and commitment to connecting with the inner knowledge and intelligence alive in every cell of our Body, Mind, and Spirit."

— Debra Oakland

Wisdom is a deep understanding — gained only by experience — of people, things, events or situations that result in the ability to choose or act to consistently produce optimum results with a minimum of time and energy. It is the ability to effectively and efficiently apply perceptions and knowledge, thereby producing the desired results. Wisdom is also the comprehension of what is true or right, coupled with optimum judgment as to appropriate action. Synonyms for wisdom include sagacity, discernment, or insight. Wisdom often requires control of one's emotional reactions (the "passions"), so that one's principles, reason, and knowledge prevail to determine one's actions. Wisdom is best gained from personal experience; however, it can be gleaned from the experiences of others. Choosing to seek wisdom and to gain wisdom is a sign of maturity and a precursor of success.

WISDOM CASTING CALL

This definition of wisdom makes me think about what it takes to write, edit, direct and produce a film. Great movie makers have to be open to new ideas and expansion. Their creativity demands it if they are to achieve the desired goal before their movie is released into the mainstream.

In the collective movie we call "Life on Earth," people are seeking wisdom through abstract perceptions and theories to gain illumination, enlightenment, and knowledge. The majority want confirmation of their own ideas, beliefs, and values. Many people do not seem to understand that true wisdom can only be gained through experience; and experience can often be challenging, forcing us to push through the resistance. What happens when a new idea that challenges one of your beliefs is presented to you? Do you want to debate because you feel you are right or because you are afraid you are not? Does your Mind slam shut as the peace of your own core ideas are disturbed, or are you open to expanding your personal movie-making skills?

Think how good it feels when you find someone or something that confirms your beliefs. People love going to a movie where the subject of the film resonates with their habits of Mind. Humans bond strongly with people of like Mind. Separation occurs when people disagree. Entire lifetimes are spent defending who is right, who is wrong. Numerous movies feature this ongoing conflict. Some of them include: *The Matrix*, the *Lord of the Rings* trilogy, the *Star Wars* series, *The Shawshank Redemption*, *Hotel Rwanda*, *Erin Brockovich*,

Saving Private Ryan and *Gandhi.* These movies show the wisdom of peace. It is my feeling these movies touch the core of who we are and what we can be when we choose to live in a state of love. Just as electrical Power results from voltage pushing against resistance, so too does wisdom result from determination staying the course in the face of challenging circumstances.

Freedom will never be won as long as everyone is trying to prove they are right, yet everyone seems to want freedom — on their terms! As each of us views life though the camera lens of wisdom, continuing to make conscious choices to live in Love and do no harm to ourselves or to others, the collective picture containing all of our individual moving pictures will continue to come into sharper and clearer focus. As your movie evolves you will be wise to live your life with integrity and honor in your pursuit of freedom.

Find out what matters to you, your truth, your purpose, because your life matters.

SELF-WISDOM

Spiritual books can be controversial, and the thought of writing one had me thinking, "What if someone does not like what I have to say?" or "Will people find value in what I write?" and any number of other ridiculous excuses I could think up. Having been an avid reader, I always dreamed of being a writer. When I thought of those who were "real" writers, I did not have the confidence that someone would want to hear what I had to say, and found myself letting go of a dream I did not see as attainable. David Icke said, "The greatest prison people live in is the fear of what other people think."

Part of confident self-growth expansion is dropping fear into the movie editing shredder. We must ask ourselves some serious questions. As the director of my life movie, are love and compassion the motivating factors? Is my life making a difference in the world? If not, how can I change my movie and change my life? What kind of wisdom can I bring into my movie-making process that will improve my life and the lives of others?

I have learned to trust my voice, which has grown with a foundation of courage. To express and share the wisdom learned throughout my life became synonymous with living in courage and creating a personal joy-filled movie. My life experiences unfold beautifully when I make choices from a place of Love. This brings endless possibilities into my experience, when I stay in alignment.

We are energy, as is everything in the Universe. Where our attention goes, energy flows. The Power of thought carries so much influence, because it creates a result. Everything we do or say or meditate upon has vibratory effects that flow out into our world. Those vibrations are molecular actions, which influence and create reactions. It is the creative force within you; that aspect of you which is "created in the image of God." As we discussed in the last chapter, we make choices constantly, whether we are aware of it or not. To be able to attain a state of awareness in which we make conscious choices in each moment is our ultimate quest. Living in a state of joy, creativity, gratitude and anticipation on a daily basis creates a vibratory resonance, attracting magnetically into our energy field more joy, creativity, gratitude and anticipation of our good.

When people, events, and places move out of your experience, is it possible this might be occurring because they are on a different energy frequency no longer matching yours? This is neither good nor bad. Nor is it to be judged. It simply is. If you learn nothing else from this book, please ponder this precept: never judge another person's path or where they are on it. No matter how well you may know another person or how long you have shared this life experience with them, you do not know what lessons are essential to their growth. You may think you know, but you might also be mistaken. Either way, you are bringing negative energy into play, and that could set off detrimental consequences and outcomes.

Share wisdom from your personal experience if it is appropriate, timely, and warranted; and from a Heart of love and compassion. If you would have freedom, you must give freedom. If you would enjoy acceptance, understanding, and compassion for yourself, you must share these qualities with others who may only be in your life for a season or are simply crossing your path. This will make you a magnet for whatever you need at the appropriate time and place you need it. Living without judgment is the first step toward true wisdom.

Letting go and moving in a different direction can be painful, but it is also the best way to serve your current and highest good. It does not mean you do not care for, or love, that with which you are no longer in synchronous vibration. It's not a match at this present time.

If we want to see positive changes occurring, one of the best ways to accomplish this is by actively participating with the Laws of Love and Peace. We are here experiencing, and as we shift, so does life. Since life is like a movie, this quote resonates with the difficult choices we sometimes have to make.

> *"Whenever you find yourself doubting how far you can go, just remember how far you have come. Remember everything you have faced, all the battles you have won, all the fears you have overcome."*
>
> — Author Unknown

ILLUMINATED WISDOM

In the movie *Avatar*, there were two worlds of complete contrast, opposing structures, beliefs and values. I feel this film shows us what is possible when we use the wisdom in our Hearts and choose to live in a state of Love. Neyteri, the princess of the Na'vi, teaches Jake the principles of Wisdom and Love. This movie provides all the great elements of action, courage, love, challenge, EGO (Editing God Out), determination and adventure — like the epic journey of our lives!

Seeing the world as broken only contributes to negative, non-healing energy. Imagine instead that this world is again pristine, healed; in a state of peace, love and joy. If we have a desire, yet doubt it can be a reality, how can that desire show up in the movie of our life? It can't. Envision this world in a state of magnificence and see it as an already-existing fact. Plant a thought seed of peace, nurturing it endlessly by your thoughts, feelings and actions.

Understanding the Universe we live and breathe in requires some basic knowledge of the working principles. Universal Laws and Principles never vary. The Universe operates on immutable laws. In the physical world, we call these rules and principles "physics." What some scientists are beginning to understand is that there is also a corresponding set of principles governing the spiritual aspects of reality. As you embrace these concepts, illuminated wisdom lights your way. Miracles do happen. Without working knowledge of the Power of inner wisdom living inside us, this Power will remain dormant until we are ready to acknowledge and claim it. A new sense of determination and purpose becomes our constant guide as we trust in the Power alive in our Hearts.

What are you thinking about during the day? Your thoughts and feelings are being directed by your attention to them. Have you ever looked through a camera lens that is out of focus? The objects are blurry, hard to see, or unrecognizable. Look through the viewfinder of your life. The parts that are in focus are clearly easy to see. If anything is out of focus or a bit blurry, get busy on some self-examination. Then refocus your efforts on giving your movie all it needs for an even more brilliant view. Acting on a desire out of fear and doubt will send you less-than-desired visuals in the camera lens. When love and joy become motivating factors in your life, the picture of the desired results in your lens can be viewed with crystal clarity.

Life is governed by immutable laws and principles that never vary. Universal Laws and Principles are present everywhere and operate in all time and space. It has been said, every effect is the result of the cause, and the effect becomes the cause, which creates other effects, and on it goes. Be vigilant, walking forward expansively in your Power. The Universe is infinite. The unseen can be brought into your reality, because there are unlimited resources available to the Universe you may not be aware of. When studying Universal Laws and Principles, one can see these are pure, uncolored concepts.

Our Perfected God Source of Divine Love and Light has no need to confirm any human ideas or beliefs. Many people pray and meditate on a desire they want to see manifested in their personal life. When it doesn't happen the way they want it to or when they want it to happen, they get discouraged and often turn negative.

What they fail to realize is what they want may not be what they need in order for them to attain the highest outcome. The Universal Laws and Principles supersede human laws and principles. They are immutable and pure in intent and motivation, leading to our eternal freedom. People who gravitate to these laws with an open Mind through the mental, spiritual, and feeling body are in a receiving mode of conceptual wisdom, putting them on the path to mental purity and emotional maturity. Application of these perfect laws is the bridge to freedom within each of us.

In *Les Misérables* we are presented with an example of this bridge in a fierce battle between dark and Light. There is a progression of evil, injustice, prejudice, corruption, lies and all manner of hidden activity which transforms into goodness, justice, truth and a transformational Soul lighting. When we are in proper orientation and allowing Love to flow through us, we get to witness the "negatives" in the movie of our own life "develop" beautifully when exposed to the Light.

How do we get to a place of inner connection and Soul satisfaction? What can we do to align our outer lives with our innermost desires? We can't. We must align ourselves to Source and allow ourselves to become a conduit through which either the physical world around us is transformed by the Power of Love or our perception of the physical world and our sensitivity to its influence are transformed. One way to accomplish this is by connecting to our Higher Self daily in sacred space, allowing the peace and wisdom gained through that connection to expand into our outer activities.

When you are still, unplugged from the outer world with inner focus, a shift occurs. As you disengage from the hustle and bustle of your world, a new perspective lights the way forward. Serenity of the Mental Body assists in calming the multi-body system (Mind, Body, Spirit). This stillness is an alert, undisturbed clarity in anticipation of your best interest, not a lazy or negative state of Mind. It is unfortunate that fear, confusion, and negativity is the daily reality for far too many people in our world today. We must daily be a positive influence in the lives of spiritually adrift people living in negativity, and lead them to Love with wisdom if we are to progress ourselves.

When you connect to this positive activity, you emerge wiser, more peaceful — ready to take on the day with confidence, aligned, and prepared through utilizing your immense inner Power. Remember, you are always present in your movie. Taking this important time to center yourself may find you responding to familiar situations in quite a different way. Listen to your Heart when in this meditative or prayerful, sacred inner space. Insights will Light you up, joy will fill you, and a renewed sense of self will emerge.

OUR INDIVIDUALIZED MASTER MOVIE DIRECTOR

Quieting the Mental Body in an alert way requires stilling your Mind and connecting to your Divine inner Source. Use whatever method feels right for you. Once this is achieved to your satisfaction, begin conversing, creating, and co-creating in this personal, sacred, inner space. Talk to the cells of your body, your DNA, the core of your being vibrating to Universal truth and clarity. This could take days, weeks or months, so if you are a new at this, be patient with yourself. The important thing is to learn to identify and listen to the quiet, calming voice speaking to you from Spirit. You won't have to guess when you hear it. It resonates with your frequency. It is different from the voice of your thoughts. It is different from the voice re-enacting an incident in the past, a story your mother told you, or last night's episode of *Law and Order.* Learn to silence all those hollow, trivial distractions competing to fill the stillness in your Soul. When you hear the voice of your Source, you will know it.

What leads to inner wisdom varies from person to person. Keep in Mind your unique, individualized path is not to be compared to another or judged in any way. After some practice, stillness of Mind will become a daily habit you eagerly anticipate.

This is where intention comes in. Choose one desire to manifest something important to you. Start with something small to practice. You will have plenty of time to work your way up to bigger things. This is to bypass any doubt your secular, cynical Mind may try to insert!

Keep your attention focused, without distractions. Of course you have a busy movie to direct, but keep your unwavering focus on this one desire as your main goal. If you are unfocused, doubt your desired outcome, or are hopping from one desire to another, your desire will be blurry and out of focus when you look through the lens of your Heart's camera, and it may never make it into your movie.

Start with something small like "Of course, I shall find a great parking spot at the store." Another one might be "I am so happy the next person to pass me on the sidewalk is going to smile back at me." After several small victories, your Mind will be convinced it works. It will start prompting you to choose to listen first to Source instead of self whenever you are faced with a choice. For instance, when the secretary says it is the head office on the phone for you, don't be surprised if the first impression you sense is "Great! They are going to give me a promotion."

It is in your best interest to choose an idea or desire not only benefiting you but all of humanity. This removes separation, placing unity center stage. We can uplift the world by being harmless to Self and others. When you take back your creative director powers, your movie will never have the same old predictable plot or performances, because you have breathed new life into it.

Do not allow any discord or doubtful ideas to interfere with the perfection of your design. Coming into alignment with Body, Mind, and Spirit works in combined harmony for you. In accepting the purity of the pattern, your idea is protected by trusting in the wisdom of your Higher Consciousness to deliver it to you in a pure state.

As you become skilled at quieting the mental chatter and listening receptively, you orient the flow of energy and enlightenment from Spirit through Self into physical manifestation. The seed idea has been planted. Once it is accepted into your Mind or consciousness, creation begins. The pattern is cut from universal Light and can bring the vague into focus, the concept into clarity, the unformed into form and substance.

An example would be the manifestation of a desire. Our feelings connect to the Mental Body to permeate the thought-form with Light in a rhythmic manner until the manifestation appears. The seventh concept in this book ties all the concepts together through rhythm.

Our feelings are extremely important, full of powerful frequencies of energy connecting to our thoughts, creating momentum. The Power of our intention, and the attention we give it, will determine how quickly we see results and how long they will last. Hold a sense of "knowing" rather than "believing." Knowing connects us powerfully to the finished form; believing carries hope, but for some, a bit of doubt. Put another way, knowingness is when the Soul sees the possibility as a shape of reality.

We are in training to become what we already are on the inside — master movie directors of Divine Love and Light. This is what we were born to be. Freedom from all we wish to overcome requires the application of Universal Laws and Principles. Within the activity of creating form, our feeling body acts as a magnet to our thoughts. This creates a bridge to the world of form or manifestation, which is the science of creation. By consciously directing our creations, the quality of our life improves.

Learn to listen to the still small voice within. The saying: "Let go, let God" speaks to surrendering to our Higher Perfected Self, knowing the perfect idea will be presented to us at the perfect time. When we are able to let go of EGO (Editing God Out), our outer self will be shown the gift our inner self (Reel God Self) wants to deliver. When this feeling comes, enjoy the awareness filling you. See it in full manifestation; this is co-creation through cooperation! Who better to be in business with than our own individualized master movie director? Learn to express daily gratitude to the master director within, whose love and attention have been on us unwaveringly, even in the midst of our lack of acknowledgment or focus on its beautiful presence.

THE ART OF LISTENING

Is listening becoming a lost art in our busy world of distractions? You will have to answer the question for yourself. Here is a little side note on the wisdom of listening, and an important note to myself as director of my own movie.

Listening is like photography.

Think of yourself as the camera. Are you on manual or auto focus? Even if you are on auto-focus, you need to know where to focus. Are you paying attention? Are you listening? Is the conversation in or out of focus? Do you find yourself distracted?

Being a good listener is learning to focus in on what is being said and discerning the context. It is important to keep your attention on the focal point or you may miss the most important nuances, just as pulling focus in a scene keeps the viewers' attention where needed. Here are some tips on communicating…

AIM, FRAME, AND FOCUS

AIM: For the speaker, don't be distracted. Have you ever been in a conversation where you are saying something you consider to be important or even heartfelt to someone, and you see their eyes wander away or even glaze over? They start looking around, and you know the conversation is OVER! Now admit it, you've done this on occasion to others. It doesn't feel good to be on either end of a polite but non-interested conversation. Conversation is a two-way street.

FRAME: One of the biggest mistakes people make when taking a photograph is failure to properly frame the picture. What do I mean? How many times have you taken the perfect candid shot of your child, your parent, your friend or someone else you care about only to notice the tree in the background looks like it is growing out of their head, or there's an overflowing dumpster in the background, or your thumb is blocking the corner of the shot? This is failure to frame the shot properly. The same holds true for conversation. Concentrate on the framework of the message the speaker is delivering. Give people a chance to speak without judgment. Who is the person speaking? What do you know of them? Have you been influenced to think positively or negatively about them? What is their perspective of the subject? Are they speaking from a position of experience, theory, or simply passing along hearsay? Do they have an agenda? Your perspective can give the take away much more value. Keep an open Mind, and you may be pleasantly surprised at what transpires.

FOCUS: On what is said. Focus the lens of your attention on the speaker. Do you understand what is being said? Do you need more clarity or have questions? Do you understand the jargon or lingo being used? If the conversation is in and out of focus, think about how to dial it in. Are you an active listener? Can you ask one question that lets the speaker know you were indeed listening? If your attention is wandering, you will have an out-of-focus conversation and will either leave the person speaking feeling uncomfortable or leave the conversation without actually understanding the important information offered to you. Don't think about how you are going to answer the question until you have actually heard the question. There may not actually be one.

We all have people in our movie now and then who never stop talking, are unwilling to listen, or are gossiping, criticizing and blaming, which makes me think of a wise mother once saying:

"We were given two ears, two eyes, and one mouth. It would be wise to use them accordingly."

Communication is a two-way street, and for effective results we need to be listening with our eyes, ears, and Heart before we speak. There is a big difference between a dialogue and a monologue. Watch people's body language; it speaks volumes on their behalf. When listening with your Heart, where the core of your stillness lives, you will notice the silence has a different language. As you become an active observer, your movie directorial skills will soar.

Our perfected self does not engage in our negativity, only in our joy. When we make a conscious effort to live in positivity daily, our perfected self has an easier job delivering Divine ideas to us for our movie.

BE A DIRECTOR OF WISDOM

Do you direct your life with wisdom? There are people in the world who do not. You will meet people who are dishonest and unkind. They lie, cheat, steal and live their life in a negative force field. As the writer, director, producer and star in the movie of your life, you don't have to deal with negative people who invite the family of fear and its cohorts to make themselves welcome on your movie set. As a director of wisdom you will want to fill your movie set with positive, kind, loving happy people. They will prove their worth to you and improve the quality of your movie.

When people talk to you, what message are they sending? Do they claim to have all the answers? Are they listeners, or are they always attempting to take over the conversation? What is going on in their life, and what is their body language conveying? Does the personal movie they are projecting back up their advice to you? Are they a living example of what you would want to do, be, or have? Do you look to people who wisely inspire without needing to be placed on a pedestal of ego? Are they living, breathing examples, true stars in the movie of their life? Whose footsteps are you following in, and why?

It is commonly said we become what we think about most, so it is advantageous to spend time with people whom we genuinely like and admire, people who are authentic, kind, loving and supportive. We cannot teach effectively that of which we have no knowledge. A wise mentor or spiritual teacher will guide us to the understanding that we hold the keys to all the answers we seek and those keys are inside us. They will escort us over the bridge to the Love, Wisdom, and Power alive in every atom and cell of our bodies. Engage with those who encourage others to live their best lives, characters who participate in your movie with joy, enthusiasm, and mutual support.

Waves of change are upon us now. To live your best life, ask what you can give, not what you can get. I recommend you read *The Go-Giver* by Bob Burg and John David Mann. This gem of a book shares five simple principles in a business parable illustrating how putting others' interests first and continually adding value to their lives — ultimately leads to unexpected returns. We are all in the "business" of life as the writer, director and producer of our movie. Feed your hopes, not your fears. Choose to ride the currents in peace, joy, and expectation. Let's direct each other to the fountain of life within and resonate to the greater good of all possibility. Listen to your Heart, trusting the answers are there for you. The Universal Laws and Principles of Life are unchangeable, offered free of charge, constant, and ever-present for our use.

> *"Correct principles do not change. We can depend on them. Principles don't react to anything. They don't get mad and treat us differently. They won't divorce us or run away with our best friend. They aren't out to get us. They can't pave our way with shortcuts and quick fixes. They don't depend on the behavior of others, the environment, or the current fad for their validity. Principles don't die. They aren't here one day and gone the next. They can't be destroyed by fire, earthquake or theft. Principles are deep, fundamental truths, classic truths, and generic common denominators. They are tightly interwoven threads running with exactness, consistency, beauty, and strength through the fabric of life."*
>
> — Stephen R. Covey
>
> *The 7 Habits of Highly Effective People*

When you direct joy into your movie production, life cooperates in turn, vibrating to your uplifted energetic frequency. What you need, when you need it, shows up at the appropriate time and place. People take notice your life is improving, as you begin living in your own self-created reality. Friends and family who witness positive changes in the different areas of your life will look to you for inspiration. You become a living example, able to direct the wisdom you have gained in positive ways.

As the peace-commanding presence, we no longer feel the need to react to triggers that used to fire us up, causing conflict. There will always be challenges, for without them there is no growth or expansion. By responding as the wise director, rather than reacting to any challenges on our movie set, we are connecting to the inner wisdom to which we have learned to attune. We can talk about our truth all day, but don't you agree living it sends a much clearer message than mere words?

You grow exponentially by connecting to your inner Power, finding yourself less concerned with the opinions of those who are not living examples of Love, Peace, and Light, because they are vibrating at a different frequency. The conflicting messages of fear in the outer world will drift away, as they will hold no credence any longer.

You will know who you are, living your truth, with no need to convince anyone you are doing the right thing. Your friends and family will take notice and, as they spend time around you, they may gain a new level of awareness to share with others. Love crosses the borders of all belief structures, and languages, because Love is who we truly are. Your mere presence, filled with Love and Light, can touch people's lives in unimaginable ways. In essence, we are a living example of all we think, feel, and act upon.

There will be people dropping out of your movie production from time to time as their part ends. Let them go. Perhaps they played their part and are moving on to a new production. Bless them for their participation with gratitude, knowing the right cast of characters will show up to audition for the parts you need filled, right when you need them.

NEW EARTH PRODUCTION

We are assisting in the birth of the New Earth Production as we raise our energetic vibrational frequency to heightened levels, acting as way-showers for a new paradigm. By daring to stand firmly in our inner Light, Love, Wisdom and authentic Power, we set the stage for a new standard of living.

What a transitional time to be on Earth! I, for one, am thrilled to be here, contributing in any way I can, in support of Love and Light. As the rules for the game of life are being redefined, our energetic blueprint will shift as this journey progresses. Our inner wisdom tells us — how strong our foundation is determines what shows up, and how stable it will remain. A weak foundation will crumble beneath our feet.

Universal Laws and Principles are Divine laws providing a solid foundation of building blocks with which to build your life. Be open to the messages, the clues, or the feelings leading you out of discord to the wisdom of inner knowing. As challenges arise, pay attention to the clues leading to new awareness. Look at the challenge presented as vibrational. A good singer can make a bad singer sound good by harmonizing in a way which takes the discordant vibration and makes it into a chord adding flavor and character. By taking responsibility for creating the challenge, we can release its hold over our life, retune the frequency, and bring new levels of awareness and wisdom into our lives. As Henry Miller said, "The full and joyful acceptance of the worst in oneself may be the only sure way of transforming it." Contrast is a masterful teacher.

LEARNING FROM MASTERS

Oprah Winfrey's Master Class Series has featured close-up personal interviews with famous people such as the late Maya Angelou, Lenny Kravitz, Susan Sarandon, Goldie Hawn, Sydney Poitier, Laird Hamilton, Ellen Degeneres and a host of many others who appeared on the *Master Class Series*. They each share the wisdom they have gained throughout their life experiences and how life has impacted and shaped them. We each have a lifetime of wisdom to share. The question is, how will we share our wisdom with others and give back with an attitude of gratitude? Giving is twofold, a gift for others and yourself.

We contribute as "actors" in the ever-changing movie roles in each other's lives. Challenges are part of life, and there is not one person who will avoid them if they are on this planet for any length of time. The wisdom we acquire and put to use will determine how we overcome these challenges. Borrowing someone else's wisdom is good if it resonates with you. We are here to share. If you ever think you don't have much to offer, think again. Wisdom comes through everyone at some point. Be open and inquisitive; ask questions, listen, and share. Allow your wisdom to reflect the wonder and creativity in you.

DEBRA'S STORYBOARD ON WISDOM

> *"We don't receive wisdom; we must discover it for ourselves after a journey that no one can take for us or spare us."*
>
> — Marcel Proust

This quote reminds me it's my journey. I must take each step; it's not up to anyone else. I am responsible for it all. For people who play the blame game, this is hard to take in. As I grew in my spiritual awareness from youth to adulthood, the evidence presented itself. I am the writer, director, and producer of my personal movie and am part of the larger collective movie. When I do my best to resonate with joy and peace, not only do I improve the vibrational quality of my life, but of all life. Here is another storyboard to begin my day.

Waking in the morning expressing gratitude starts the day out right for me. Choosing Love and Light over fear brings us closer to the wisdom we all seek. I use different mental practices I have found work for me and would like to share one related to wisdom I find very effective.

I imagine myself engulfed in white Light for a few minutes. I then visualize the Light as it emanates in, through and around every cell of my body. This Light is joyous, filled with the wisdom of the Universe. I feel it pulsing from the inside out, which always brings a smile to my face. I then connect with the sacred space within my Heart.

I see the flames of Love, Wisdom, and Power expanding in my chest cavity. I see pink, violet/blue, and golden Light I connect with in love and gratitude. I then visualize these flames much like a fleur-de-lis, expanding as they flow through my entire body like a fountain.

I continue to visualize and feel the energy of this combined Light expanding out from me in a circle of beautiful, golden Light shimmering with the soft pink and violet/blue.

When I feel complete stillness, it is as if the world slips softly away. I sit immersed in love as I absorb the beauty of each moment. This powerful connection with my Source of All Good, the God/Goddess within, begins my day in a more relaxed and peaceful manner.

YOUR PERSONAL STORYBOARD ON WISDOM

1. Upon awakening in the morning, I consciously and purposely use Wisdom to focus upon:

____

____

____

____

____

2. In my personal daily spiritual ritual, I acknowledge my truth or purpose to be:

____

____

____

____

____

3. By aligning Mind with Spirit, I recognize I have gained Wisdom from:

____

____

____

____

____

4. As I start my daily walk, I shall focus my intention upon:

____

____

____

____

____

5. One thing I can freely give to people I meet is:

6. In Light and Love, I recognize and acknowledge these principles operating in my life:

7. The negative frequencies I choose to change with Love and Wisdom are:

#2 — TREATMENT FOR SCRIPT ON WISDOM

FADE IN:

A young girl named Ellen finds herself dissatisfied with her life. At the age of 16, she feels life is not turning out the way she had wanted.

She sees girls at school who she thinks are prettier than she, wear more stylish clothes than her parents can afford, hang out with the best looking boys, and seem to be having a great time in school. This makes her confidence level drop when she passes them in the hallway. Everything in the outer world they seem to have, she feels she is lacking. She knows her self-confidence needs a boost and tells herself,

"If only I was like those girls and had the things they have, I would feel better, be more popular, and be happy. My world would be perfect!"

One day she stumbles over an old lantern on her way home from school. She rubs it to see if it will shine and — POOF! — a genie appears!

"Because you have freed me from the lamp in which I was imprisoned," says the genie, "I shall grant you one wish. Whatever your Heart desires, whatever your Mind can conceive, it shall be yours. What do you desire, Memsahib?"

Ellen does not stop to think before she speaks.

"I want a complete makeover of my life!" she exclaims. "I want to be the prettiest, most popular girl in school, wear the latest designer clothes, have all the money I can spend, and generally rule the school with my fabulous self!"

"As you wish," says the genie. He snaps his fingers and, instantly, Ellen's life is transformed.

Now there is nothing wrong with any of these qualities in and of themselves; but in Ellen's case, her orientation was reversed. Ego had taken control of her Heart and Mind. Her perception of reality was flowing from the external physical world outside her, toward her inner self. External stimulation was creating negative energy flow, and she lost sight of reality and embraced an illusion.

As she walks into school the next morning, all eyes are on Ellen. Everyone smiles and gives her compliments. At first, she thanks them, by lunch she is agreeing with them. All the boys want to sit with her and tell her how hot and sexy she is. Girls who were once her closest friends ask to sit with her, and she sends them away, telling them not to bother her anymore.

"Can't you see how popular I am? How beautiful I've become?" says Ellen, waving her hands at the infatuated gaggle of guys surrounding her.

"All I can see," says one of her oldest friends, "is what a conceited, arrogant phony you've become."

One by one, her friends move away from her in the lunch room. The boys begin to get bored when Ellen starts telling them about the designer outfit she has on and where she is going on her European vacation over spring break. By the end of lunch, she is sitting alone. By the end of the day, nobody is talking to her. Nobody is looking at her. She has everything she thought would make her happy, but now she is alone. Nobody wants to be her friend. Nobody likes her. She tells herself they are jealous, but she knows it isn't true. She becomes confused and resentful. Resentment leads to anger and bitterness. She goes on a spending spree, but that doesn't help.

She becomes depressed and begins self-medicating with drugs and alcohol. She becomes promiscuous, thinking she will find love and acceptance through sex; but everyone uses her and leaves her alone again. Nothing works. Nothing is ever enough. She has it all, and she isn't happy. It isn't fair!

Soon she is trying to stay loaded all the time. Her grades nosedive. She begins tearing up and burning her clothes. She begins cutting herself. She feels numb. Her parents try to help her with therapy and rehab. She learns to deceive them by pretending she is feeling better and ready to return home; but, within a matter of days, she is back out partying with strangers; out of control and often gone for days.

One morning, Ellen's mother opens the front door to find two police officers standing on the front porch.

"We're sorry, ma'am, but your daughter Ellen was apparently partying with some people…."

FADE TO BLACK

#2 — REWRITE OF TREATMENT FOR SCRIPT ON WISDOM

FADE IN:

A young girl named Ellen finds herself dissatisfied with her life. At the age of 16, she feels life is not turning out the way she had wanted.

She sees girls at school who she thinks are prettier than she, wear more stylish clothes than her parents can afford, hang out with the best looking boys, and seem to be having a great time in school. This makes her confidence level drop when she passes them in the hallway. Everything in the outer world they seem to have, she feels she is lacking. She knows her self-confidence needs a boost and tells herself,

"If only I was like those girls and had the things they have, I would feel better, be more popular, and be happy. My world would be perfect!"

One day she stumbles over an old lantern on her way home from school. She rubs it to see if it will shine and — POOF! — a genie appears!

"Because you have freed me from the lamp in which I was imprisoned," says the genie, "I shall grant you one wish. Whatever your Heart desires, whatever your Mind can conceive, it shall be yours. What do you desire, Memsahib?"

Ellen stops to think before she speaks.

She has learned from experience not to answer a question or grab an opportunity before considering all the possibilities. She remembers her mother's words at her fifth birthday party.

"Be careful what you wish for, because you just might get it."

After some careful consideration, she asks the patiently waiting genie, "I can have anything I want?"

"Whatever you desire in your Heart or conceive in your Mind," answers the genie. "It is within my Power to see to it you have exactly what you wish for."

Ellen thinks for a moment, and then she smiles at the genie.

"I wish to be able to realize my full potential and to become all I was born to be," she says.

"A wise choice, Memsahib," beams the genie. "As you wish!"

He snaps his fingers and vanishes. Ellen notices she feels better. She is happy and confident. She suddenly feels the overwhelming need to start writing down some goals for her life. As she writes, she begins to expound on each goal and her list grows into a journal. She expands her daily entries to include events of the day, her thoughts about them, and the lessons learned from the experience. She notices a clarity and purpose in her thoughts.

Her friends at school see she appears happier and has a quiet confidence. They remark they enjoy her company and like her because she is real. She thanks them sincerely and encourages them at every opportunity. Her popularity begins to grow, and people feel drawn to her, even the girls who had previously snubbed her.

She begins to notice correlations between subjects she is studying and what is going on in the world. She finds the subjects interesting and tries to figure out how each one helps build a foundation for the plan she is creating for her life. Her teachers note her rising confidence and begin calling on her more in class. Her grades rise, and her friends begin asking her to help them with their homework. Soon, she is being paid to tutor other students and saving money for college.

By the time she graduates, she is valedictorian and is offered a full scholarship from her favorite university. She goes on to graduate with honors, earns a graduate degree, and receives a great job offer right out of school with an international, non-governmental agency. They have taken notice of papers she has published and recognize her perspective brings wisdom and understanding beyond her years with respect to the issues upon which they are working.

One morning, Ellen's mother opens the door to find Ellen and a handsome young gentleman standing on the front porch.

"Good morning, Mother. This is William. He is the man I told you about meeting at the conference in Vienna last year. William, this is my mother, Marie."

"I am delighted to meet you, Marie," smiles William as he takes Marie's hand. "Ellen has told me so much about you and your husband. I feel like I already know you."

FADE TO WHITE

REEL WRAP: THE CONCEPT OF WISDOM

★ Keep an open Mind. View life through the camera lens of wisdom.

★ Still the Mind to learn the "Art of Listening." Communication is a two-way street, and for effective results, listen with your eyes, ears, and Heart before you speak.

★ When you are able to let go of EGO (Editing God Out), your outer self will be shown the gift your inner self (Reel God Self) wants to deliver.

★ You cannot teach effectively what you are not. A wise mentor or spiritual teacher will guide you to the understanding that you hold the keys to all the answers you seek and those keys are inside you.

★ To live your best life, ask what you can give, not what you can get. Feed your hopes, not your fears.

★ Become a vibratory match to what you want to experience in your life. Making choices to support your life movie will magnetize to you what you need, at the appropriate time and place.

★ Take responsibility for creating the challenges appearing in your life. This creates a healing, releasing the hold which particular challenges seem to have over your life.

Concept #3: LOVE

What's Love Got to Do with It?

"When the waters of life want to carry us back into the arms of Divine Love and Light, we must not cling to the shore in fear."

— Debra Oakland

BECOME A LOVE MAGNET

The word love carries the highest of vibrations. Love is a concentrated, positive, magnetic quality in every human Heart. The Heart generates the largest electromagnetic field produced in the body. As we shift our emotions, we are changing the information encoded into the electromagnetic fields radiated by the Heart. This is music to my ears, because as we are feeling emotions such as love, gratitude, and peace, the Heart beats out a positive message. The movies that so deeply touch our Hearts and souls contain a variety of themes revolving around love, and our Hearts respond. Love has the capacity to heal, removing deeply embedded wounds from our life.

"To love very much is to love inadequately; we love — that is all. Love cannot be modified without being nullified. Love is a short word, but it contains everything. Love means the body, the soul, the life, the entire being. We feel love as we feel the warmth of our blood; we breathe love as we breathe the air; we hold it in ourselves as we hold our thoughts. Nothing more exists for us. Love is not a word; it is a wordless state indicated by four letters."

— Guy de Maupassant

Have you noticed when people feel love intensely, the rest of the world falls temporarily into the background? Joy fills the Heart and happiness prevails. The motivating factor for change or shifts to occur in our personal lives, and out in the world, is love. How can we expect to overcome limiting experiences if we aren't open to releasing old patterns no longer benefiting our life? We are attuned and aligned toward attracting through The Law of Love as we daily release all that is not love and allow in all that is love. We begin to reorient our focus toward being in the moment, attuned to those around us.

Think of The Law of Love as nutrition for the Body, Mind, and Spirit — nourishing fuel determining the health of our inner and outer lives, giving us the strength, wisdom, and power to live the life we picture for ourselves. The Law of Love contains within it all the great qualities of life. If we want its benefits, participation and cooperation are required. Letting go of our unwanted and all too predictable Egocentric performances makes room for new possibilities, probabilities, and heartfelt characterizations to fill the spaces and places we have cleared. Out with the old; in with the new! The ultimate goal is growth of happiness and the healthy expansion of all that brings us joy.

Challenges will occur, bringing with them opportunities for growth making us stronger, more resilient, and better equipped to handle every ad lib life sends our way. I have been faced with many opportunities in my life requiring me to improvise. I have found performing from a place of Love serves to save the scene. When I respond from a centered place of Love, I am allowing the flow of the Light of Love to illuminate the situation and spotlight the need. When the response comes from the Love of the Heart before the analysis and critique of the Mind, the emotion is calming and the words are healing. There is not one person who gets through life without varying degrees of difficulty. How we learn to handle challenges determines the quality of our life.

Learn the art of living and loving. Step out of mediocrity to embrace the expansive change living in the flow of Love offers. Eliminate the facade of FEAR. It is an acronym — False Evidence Appearing Real. It is where all of your excuses originate, blinding you to the reality of the moment. It is an illusion, usually created by Self to avoid taking responsibility or being proactive. Paulo Coelho's powerful quote is also applicable here.

> *"Difficulty: the name of an ancient tool that was created purely to help us define who we are."*

An example is when you enter a new situation and your Mind

tells you that you are not worthy of other people liking you. This is not real, it is not even realistic. You do not have enough information to know whether or not people will like you. It is a false assumption with no basis in fact.

The fact you are a Divine being capable of giving and receiving love, joy, and happiness means you are, by default, worthy. Not only is it more likely people will like you, because you ARE a new actor in their scene, some will even come to love you as they get to know who you really are. Tear down the facade of FEAR. Embrace hope, exude joy, and trust Love. The biggest risk in life is to risk nothing at all.

IS A WONDERFUL LIFE IN YOUR FUTURE?

How does love fit into our decision-making, you may ask? You and I are more in control of our lives than we realize. We are a projection of what we think, say, and do. What we focus our Mind on becomes our reality because of our perception. We are creating our movie before we even take action! If our perception is that life is unfair and people cannot be trusted, we should not act surprised when others avoid interaction with us. One of our most underutilized talents is our ability to sense what is going on with another person. If it is something negative, we are instinctively guarded. If it is warm and positive, we are attracted. This is why making choices in and around love propels us into our best movie-making roles.

The classic movie *It's a Wonderful Life*, starring Jimmy Stewart as

George Bailey, is about a perpetual do-gooder on Christmas Eve who finds himself in a terrible predicament through no fault of his own. In a desperate moment of suicidal self-pity, he wishes he had never been born. His somewhat inept and wingless guardian angel, Clarence, gives him the opportunity to find out how important his life has been. He gets to see how much he mattered in the lives of his family and friends in Bedford Falls and what their lives would have looked like without him. He discovers people who gather together for the greater good, in a spirit of Love and guided by Light, make a great deal of difference. They even have the Power to foil the evil plans of others, as George discovers in this magical movie. In the process of learning and embracing this lesson, George helps Clarence finally earn his wings!

Think about how different this world would be if you had never been born. Each one of us has, at some time, made a positive difference in someone else's life. We may not even have been aware of it at the time. It may have been something as seemingly insignificant as a smile, a kind word, or holding the door open for someone. This small act of kindness could have had enough force of Love behind it to change the course of their life by one degree.

You may, as I did, be asking yourself, "What difference does one degree of course change make?" Let me give you an example. Imagine you set off in a sailboat from Los Angeles to Hawaii with only a compass to guide you. You leave from Marina del Rey aboard your 46-foot sailboat and you manage to hold a steady bearing of 260.38 degrees. About 18 days and 2,540 miles later, you drop anchor off the town of Kailua on the island of Oahu in Hawaii.

If you had adjusted your course by just one degree to the north upon leaving Los Angeles, you would have sailed through the Ka`ie`ie Waho Channel between Oahu and Kauai, 14 miles from the closest land. Your next landfall would be about four weeks later on the Ontong Java Atoll, 200 miles northeast of Choiseul in the Solomon Islands and 5,967 miles from California!

What we do in our lives matters much more than we realize. One act of kindness done in the spirit of Love can make a one-degree course correction in a person's life. A one degree change can, over several moments, make the difference in a person reaching their desired destination or sailing along aimlessly, exhausting their resources and ending up nowhere. When Love is the basis for every choice we make in our life, we can change the world, even if only by degrees. Taking responsibility with love as a focus puts you in control as the director in the movie of your life.

HOW MUCH DO YOU LOVE YOURSELF?

Life comes from us, not at us. It makes sense Love is the meaning of life and should become the spotlight on your movie set. More love brings more Light and illuminates the world around us. In the movie *Forrest Gump*, it is said life is like a box of chocolates because you never know what you're going to get. Sure there are surprises, but we get to choose our experiences. Some will be delicious and easy to swallow, others you will discard after one small bite, because they don't appeal to your taste. We've all made choices that did not taste good, yet through the trial and error of choosing, we gained courage and built up levels of strength and depth of character we would not have had otherwise.

If your life is perfect all the time, I applaud you, but most of us have a few bitter chocolates in the mix. By being tested and experiencing contrast, we expand, grow, and learn to sharpen our chocolate preferences.

Learning to love ourselves is essential to loving others. This takes conscious action on our part. We can't decide to love others while we are beating ourselves up; it doesn't work that way! We must take the appropriate steps to "Be Loving" in all areas in our lives. In taking responsibility for our life, self-love and acceptance is an important element. The great actress and comedian, Lucille Ball said: "Love yourself first and everything else falls into line. You really have to love yourself to get anything done in this world."

It is important to love yourself. In the way a parent loves their child, we must love ourselves to become fully actualized in this life. We must provide for our basic physical necessities: shelter, clothing, and healthy nourishing food and water. We must provide for our emotional needs: maintaining a balanced outlook, thinking of others, and learning the Power of humility. We must provide for our own spiritual needs: connecting to the God of our knowing, spending time in nature, being mindful of what we feed our Mind, and living in a state of gratitude.

With true love of self comes self-guidance, self-correction, and the ability to exercise self-discipline when needed. We must gain through experience the discernment to avoid toxic situations and relationships. It is your life; you have the right to decide who gets to share your time and your journey. You won't live a long and happy life if all you do is hang out in a back street dive drinking cheap whiskey and chain-smoking cigarettes. The same principle applies to the emotional and spiritual aspects of your life. You must protect yourself from any situation or relationship not beneficial and mutually supportive.

A golden rule to ponder: when denying love of your Self, you are denying love to others, placing yourself on the path to imbalance. In accepting ourselves and actively loving who we are and who we are capable of becoming, we evolve. In denial of this love, we flail around in darkness. This is a path that invariably leads to falling into the whirlpool of self-pity and getting swallowed into a dark hole devoid of Light. The less love you allow into your life, starting with love of yourself, the more likely you are to fall into depression. When we learn to love and accept ourselves unconditionally, we give ourselves permission to silence the negative inner critic, Ego.

By placing love outside ourselves, we are feeding the disillusion of discord that has been upon the Earth for a very long time. By loving ourselves and others, by feeding every part of our Body, Mind, and Spirit with a reality of happiness, we are participating in moving this planet Earth back toward Source at an accelerating pace. By loving yourself, you are acting in harmony with the Universe.

A friend of mine recently said, "Love people when they are least lovable, because that's when they need it most." She told me about dealing with someone she cared deeply for, who continually blamed their self-created reality on others. With the understanding her friend needed positivity, loving support, and guidance to see the true Source of the negativity, there was a positive turnaround and a happy ending to the story. Some of the most difficult moments in our life have the potential to open our eyes and our Hearts. Whenever we withhold love from anyone, we withhold love from everyone, including ourselves.

WAKE FROM THE ILLUSION

> *"Your vision will become clear only when you can look into your own heart. Who looks outside, dreams; who looks inside, awakens."*
>
> — Carl Jung

You need only look inside your Heart to awaken from the illusion of all that limits you. Listen closely to the still, small voice within, which provides you with opportunities to tap into your inner powerhouse of knowledge. When we deny our personal Power, others seem to have more in the "outside" world. This can pull us in until we find ourselves living from the "outside in." Living from the "inside out" is the wiser choice keeping us connected to our Heart center, the true Source of our Power. Internal change must precede external change.

Once we accept, embrace, and tap into our inner personal Power, we always have what we need, when we need it. When we deny our innate goodness or fight against our higher purpose, we abandon ourselves on a dark street corner of life, exposed and vulnerable. It isn't long before Selfish Ego shows up to taunt us, as it is antagonistic, demanding, and enjoys the act of seduction. Selfish Ego wants what it does not have, whether needed or not, whether healthy or not. Selfish Ego vies for your attention. Once it gets it, there is a good chance it will pull you into its grip.

In the book *A Journey to Oneness*, by Rasha it states, "Everything present in your awareness is a reflection of your own state of beingness. Quell the turbulent seas of the ego-self. This is simply a movie, playing out a symbolic representation of a set of vibrational variables, for the reference of a pinpoint of consciousness."

One of those immutable Laws of the Universe is: you attract whatever you focus your attention upon, whether positive or negative. Whenever Selfish Ego whispers in your ear, turn away and focus your attention toward the ultimate love of Source. Withdraw your attention from its negative thoughts, build an arsenal of love and positivity, and watch as the undesirable things it has brought into your life fade away.

Does this mean you will not have any challenges? No, but they show up less often, and your ability to handle them will improve. Once the key is turned to the door of our spiritual Heart of Love and Light, we will find more doors to our good opening. Love unlocks doors nothing else can pry open. Examples of this powerful magnetic force are everywhere.

Love is the essence of who we are. Connecting with the love present in our Heart and Soul is the most powerful force in the Universe, capable of transforming anything. The best thing is, when we are committed to loving ourselves, the love we find to complement our life is that much better, stronger, and lasting. Opening our Hearts to love is like opening the windows in a dark room and allowing Light to shine in. There are corners of our lives that may be lying in the darkness. We control whether these areas will remain dark forever or will be flooded with Light.

Altering the lighting in a movie changes the scene. Holding back Light sets the tone for a darker movie. Radiating bright Light sets the tone for an entirely different movie experience. By shining Light into the dark corners of our life, we can change our movie and our life.

Anticipating miracles and manifestations to come into your life is a beautiful thing. Carry your expectation to the God/Goddess of Love alive in you, trusting the all-knowing Personalized Power in you to handle the details. Your work is to control your thoughts, see your desires in full living color, take the action steps necessary, and allow the process to continue in perfect order. Imagine the excellent results you could anticipate and get.

Living from the outside in without tapping into this powerful inner presence can lead to disappointment when we expect things from people in the outer world often not delivered. One of the best ways to direct your Love Movie is to become a lover of people. You become a love magnet in return.

Do you have the courage to open your Heart when confronted with darkness or to risk rejection from people who are not ready to step into their own Light or even to step up and share yours? What's the worst that could happen if you put yourself out there to shine your Light? Find out by sending an invitation to your movie premiere featuring LOVE, knowing your movie may not yet appeal to all audiences.

> *"There are only four questions of value in life, Don Octavio. What is sacred? Of what is the spirit made? What is worth living for, and what is worth dying for? The answer to each is the same — only love."*
>
> — Jeremy Leven
>
> Screenwriter of *Don Juan DeMarco*

How do the many qualities of love demonstrate themselves in the different scenes in your movie? Is the moving picture of your life a classic love story with some comedy thrown in or a suspense drama filled with surprises? What qualities of life are showing up in your relationships, work, or home? Do you inspire trust, integrity, peace, respect, compassion and forgiveness in others? Is your life balanced to your satisfaction or out of sync in certain areas? If you think negatively or feel defeated, limited, and unworthy, you will be. How we demonstrate love or non-love in our life mirrors right back to us.

Our consciousness cannot act on a mixed thought or feeling. When you say yes to love, love says YES to you. The Universe says yes to anything you set your Mind to, as does your subconscious Mind.

In truth, in the presence of love, you are never alone. Connect with your Heart each day and bask in the Love in you. When you choose a soundtrack for the movie of your life, make sure it exemplifies the true nature of your expression of Love.

PAY LOVE FORWARD COURAGEOUSLY

When courage is required, consider letting your courageous intention be love. We all have personal stories. I don't know one person who has not gone through challenges in one or more areas of their life. As we grow stronger and wiser from overcoming each obstacle with grace, love, and peace, we lay claim to our victorious life. As a momentum of confidence and knowingness is built, we move farther away from negative influences, into a space of positivity.

Empower others with loving support. Encourage them to embrace love. Participate in it with others. Spread it around by paying it forward. In the movie *Pay It Forward,* Trevor, an eleven-year-old boy, is given a class assignment by his social studies teacher to devise a plan of action that will change the world for the better. He decides that networking good deeds would be a perfect way to "Pay It Forward" and so names his project. Trevor does favors for three people, asking each to pay the favor forward to three other people. No favor is paid back to the recipient but goes out to create a branching tree of goodwill. Each person is told it needs to be a major favor the recipient can't complete for themselves. We surely could change the world if we all helped each other in this way. Until the time of unity arrives, pay forward what you can, where you can, knowing you make a difference in the bigger picture.

BECOME A JEDI MASTER OF LOVE & LIGHT

Who better than you to become the master of your life? Let your Light saber of love cut through the fear and doubt you wish to eliminate. Allow the force of love and peace to fill your consciousness and filter your perceptions. Our senses are there to guide us, creating an open door to our consciousness canvas, where we can paint ourselves a masterpiece exemplifying the theme of our movie. Many have lived through a real life Star Wars of sorts, and by choosing the Light, we bring harmonious activity into our creations, helping us release limitation. The magnetic Power of our Heart connects us to our desire, drawing it to us at the appropriate time. This is the path of the Jedi Master!

Patience, young Jedis of Love! What we decide to be, we will be. Our world is one of creation, and we are here to create from all the qualities of Love. When we are in alignment, doors open to guide and assist our Heart's journey; being out of alignment brings less-than-desired results. When making life choices in alignment with your internal guidance system, you support your highest good, moving forward with positive momentum. Ask yourself, "What do I want the outcome in the movie of my life to be if I make this particular choice or decision?"

It's a Wonderful Life and other movies centered on "choice" remind us the Power to choose is ours. To assure the best outcome in your personal movie script, choose love as your movie-making guide. This prepares you to direct and command your thoughts and feelings into camera-ready action! Love has no borders. Love does not care what color, nationality, race or sex we are. Love just is. Divine Love is unconditional love — simply said, Love without conditions. What a wonderfully joyous day it will be when we all remember we are simply love. All the rest is an illusion being played out to bring us back to love, home to our Hearts, the place we can rest in peace.

How does love affect our Earth and its inhabitants? The ongoing conversation around the world is that our existence on Earth is threatened. We are in the midst of metamorphosis on our journey back to unity. Mother Earth supports us in Love and Light, yet she has not been given equal care and love in return. She deserves our greatest respect and appreciation for the gifts she and her kingdoms of nature provide.

Our personal choices have collectively brought us to where we are now. What we see in the outer world shows the cause and effects of our actions. The vibrational energy of the Earth creates change in our lives as these frequencies continue to shift and accelerate. Yes, we have been injured, in pain, and have suffered in life at some point, but there is a tipping point when all of it can be released and healed. The same is true for Mother Earth; she is at a tipping point. We have witnessed her cleansing through cataclysms in the past. For those of us living on her surface, our mental and physical bodies can become overloaded, making it a challenge to receive the nutrition Love and Light provide. There is a beautiful movie short, *Through the Lens of the Camera,* by contributing author, Steve Tallamy, at the end of the book. Steve's "Nature Interludes" beautifully exemplifies the power of

Mother Earth and her kingdoms as he ties in the 7 Reel Concepts throughout the book. It is important to have Steve's movie as a stand-alone piece of cinematic perfection. As Steve will tell you, there is an urgent need for healing. Love and Light will spiral us and our Earth upward in the ongoing ascension process; fear causes a downward spiral, which can have dire consequences.

Negativity and discord will continue to visit in an attempt to be released by the great intelligence within our Hearts. Positivity and joy open the door to the clearing process, bringing healing to many areas of our personal life and our world. When the old energy of Selfish Ego suddenly and unexpectedly shows up, remember it is there to divert your focus and thwart your positive love force. If you have a tendency to stuff the old energy of those feelings down, which will come up at another time, this is the perfect opportunity for healing and forgiveness. You and I have the choice to look at Selfish Ego and say, "I hear you. I see you. I feel you. I love you for the contrast you offer, but you are now no longer the focus of my attention. I shine Light on you and release you out of my life forever."

Your experiences with people will trigger situations in the exact energized concentration you put into it. If there is an experience you have disconnected from and not brought to peace, it can show up and blindside you. Release judgment, blame, and the band of critics from your movie. Give yourself the opportunity to forgive and release these past situations into Love and Light for transformation.

You and I are living Light, vibrational beings, as is all of creation.

The Earth changes now upon us will be easier to handle as we transition, accepting the Love and Light freely available to everyone. As Mother Earth is shifting into new vibrational frequencies, we can spend some quality time in appreciation and loving support of Mother Earth and her kingdoms, letting her know we understand she is going through great shifts, and we are willing to make those shifts with her. Hafiz sums it up in this quote:

> *"Even after all this time,*
> *The sun never says to the earth,*
> *'You owe me.'*
> *Look what happens with*
> *A love like that.*
> *It lights the whole sky."*

DEBRA'S STORYBOARD ON LOVE

> *"Being deeply loved by someone gives you strength, while loving someone deeply gives you courage."*
>
> — Lao Tzu

Self-love is essential to inner happiness. I connect with my Heart, directing and allowing love to flow into every area of my Body, Mind, and Spirit. Cleansing my energy field is a daily activity, when I wake and before sleep.

As I move into sacred space, the vibrant colors and sounds of a tropical forest wash over me. I visualize myself standing under a massive waterfall in a beautiful forest of deep green, and as the waters of purification flow over me, I feel all concerns I am carrying released and transformed. I dive into the water with a feeling of weightless freedom. Stepping out of the water, I stand in a pillar of brilliant white Light; the cells of my body Light up like a starry night expanding brilliantly in, through, and out from me.

The next step is to feel loving acceptance and appreciation of myself just the way I am, regardless of appearances, because in the bigger picture, I am so much more than my physical body. Learning to love and accept myself as I am is an ongoing process I continue to work on daily. Unconditional love starts with me, because if I do not love myself as I am, I am taking something valuable from myself and others.

Love without conditions....not an easy task! It is a work in progress each day leading me to higher ground, and I must tell you, it feels good! Gratitude is my priority. When I remain in loving appreciation for all the good in my life and out in the world, life says yes, yes, yes! This statement on love and wisdom inspires me to be still, let go, and trust in God to handle the details.

> *"Be still. Be still. Be still. God in the midst of you is substance. God in the midst of you is love. God in the midst of you is wisdom. Let not your thoughts be given to lack, but let wisdom fill them with the substance and faith of God.*
>
> *Let not your heart be a center of resentment and fear and doubt. Be still and know that at this moment it is*

the altar of God, of love; love so sure and unfailing, love so irresistible and magnetic that it draws your supply to you from the great storehouse of the universe.

Trust God, use God's wisdom, prove and express God's love."

— Myrtle Fillmore

YOUR PERSONAL STORYBOARD ON LOVE

1. Upon awakening in the morning, I consciously direct Love toward:

____

____

____

____

____

2. In my personal daily spiritual ritual, I express gratitude for:

____

____

____

____

____

3. By aligning Mind with Spirit, I allow Love to flow through me toward:

4. In my daily walk, I shall change the world one degree at a time by:

5. When life comes at me, I will respond by choosing:

6. One of the immutable principles of the Universe operating in my life is:

____

____

____

____

____

7. Today, I release Love and forgiveness toward:

____

____

____

____

____

#3 — TREATMENT FOR SCRIPT ON LOVE

FADE IN:

A ten-year-old boy is expected to become the head of a household when his dad leaves one day. He cannot understand what has happened, and there is nobody to explain it to him. His mom is withdrawn into a shell of self-pity. His baby sister is scared and won't stop crying. He doesn't understand why his dad left without saying goodbye, and he tries to figure out what he could have done differently that would have made his dad stay. The boy does not have any answers but knows somehow it is his fault.

He keeps thinking his dad will come back. Then one day he hears his dad has married another woman and has started a new family with her. His dad has other children who seem to be more important to him than the ones he left behind. He sees his mom becoming sadder, and there is nothing he can do to make it all better. He comes to realize he can never fill his dad's shoes or the void he feels in his Heart.

As the boy grows into a young adult, he learns to act happy on the outside but keeps his Heart closely guarded. He does not want to experience a repeat performance of his own childhood. He meets an amazing young woman one night at a local coffee house. He feels something in his Heart he hasn't felt since he was a young boy: happiness and hope. They begin to date, and he discovers she is everything he has ever dreamed the perfect girl would be. She is kind, loving, intelligent, fun, beautiful, and passionate; but he is afraid to tell her how he feels.

She, on the other hand, sees him for the man he is capable of being. She is open and honest about her feelings toward him. She tells him she loves him. After a few months, she begins to talk about marriage and having a family. He finds himself gripped with panic at the thought of becoming a dad. He begins to feel the empty pain he hasn't felt in years and remembers that dads leave and desert their families. He knows he can never be a good father, because he never experienced what a good father was supposed to be.

He slowly begins to withdraw, undermining and unraveling the relationship out of fear. He suddenly ends it and moves on: a pattern he will repeat many times in his life, never accepting the love he truly deserves.

FADE TO BLACK

#3 — REWRITE OF TREATMENT FOR SCRIPT ON LOVE

FADE IN:

A ten-year-old boy is expected to become the head of a household when his dad leaves one day. He cannot understand what has happened, and there is nobody to explain it to him. His mom is withdrawn into a shell of self-pity. His baby sister is scared and won't stop crying. He doesn't understand why his dad left without saying goodbye, and he tries to figure out what he could have done differently that would have made his dad stay. The boy does not have any answers but knows somehow it is his fault.

He keeps thinking his dad will come back. Then one day he hears his dad has married another woman and has started a new family with her. His dad has other children who seem to be more important to him than the ones he left behind. He sees his mom becoming sadder, and there is nothing he can do to make it all better. He comes to realize he can never fill his dad's shoes or the void he feels in his Heart.

As the boy grows into a young adult, he learns to act happy on the outside but keeps his Heart closely guarded. He does not want to experience a repeat performance of his own childhood. He meets an amazing young woman one night at a local coffee house. He feels something in his Heart he hasn't felt since he was a young boy: happiness and hope. They begin to date, and he discovers she is everything he has ever dreamed the perfect girl would be. She is kind, loving, intelligent, fun, beautiful and passionate; but he is afraid to tell her how he feels.

She, on the other hand, sees him for the man he is capable of being. She is open and honest about her feelings toward him. She tells him she loves him. After a few months, she begins to talk about marriage and having a family.

The young man feels an old fear start to rise up inside him, but he decides if this beautiful person is so willing to express her love for him, then he must be worthy of feeling loved. He opens up to her about growing up without a father and how it made him feel. He tells her he is not sure he knows how to be a good dad and all about his fear of failing.

She takes his hand and explains to him not everyone abandons their loved ones, nor is a child prepared to understand the circumstances around such loss. She tells him his willingness to be open to true love, Love of the Heart and Soul, indicates he is a man of substance who would never abandon his family. She tells him that even though he does not understand the pain he has carried around for so long, he must forgive his dad for leaving and his mom for not protecting him as she gave into the deep sadness that debilitated their family.

CUT TO:

Five years later, he and his wife are celebrating the birth of their first child. As he holds his newborn baby boy, he promises his son he will always be there for him. He tells his boy how much he loves him and loves his mommy and how they are going to have a warm and happy home. As he places his newborn son back into the arms of his mother, she looks up at him with tears in her eyes and tells him how proud she is of him and how much she loves him.

"I love you too, my angel," he tells her. "I love both of you more than I can ever express. You have made me the happiest man in the world."

FADE TO WHITE

REEL WRAP: THE CONCEPT OF LOVE

★ Love has the capacity to heal, removing deeply embedded wounds from your life.

★ When the response comes from the Love of the Heart before the analysis and critique of the Mind, the emotion is calming and the words are healing.

★ Eliminate the facade of FEAR. It is an acronym — False Evidence Appearing Real

★ The fact you are a Divine being capable of giving and receiving love, joy, and happiness means you are, by default, worthy.

★ When love is the basis for every choice you make in your life, you can change the world; even if only by degrees.

★ With true love of self comes self-guidance, self-correction, and the ability to exercise self-discipline when needed.

★ One of the immutable Laws of the Universe is that you attract whatever you focus your attention upon, whether positive or negative.

Concept #4: PURITY

What Kind of Diamonds Are We Talking about Here?

"Simply by being your true authentic self, you gift the world with your presence."

Debra Oakland

DIAMONDS ARE A GIRL'S BEST FRIEND

In the 1953 film *Gentlemen Prefer Blondes,* Marilyn Monroe sang, "Diamonds Are a Girl's Best Friend." In fact, Monroe's rendition of the song has been considered an iconic performance, copied by many entertainers. She was not the first to perform it, but her version of the song is by far the most popular. Another fun fact is the song was listed as the 12th most important song of all time by the American Film Institute. Imagine that!

I enjoyed the film and have no problem wearing diamonds, but the main objective here is to talk about another important aspect of this beautiful gemstone. Diamonds are considered a symbol of purity. We are like multifaceted diamonds in the rough, and sometimes we need a good purity polish. Diamonds can be contaminated by very few types of impurities and are one of the most sought-after and most valued gemstones. They also have a high dispersion of Light and are lovely to look at. Diamonds are believed by many to enhance one's inner vision and intuitive connection with the Divine.

Most diamonds contain some inner flaws, like we do. These flaws occur during the formation process, as do ours during our "life" formation process. There are many types of diamonds. Different colors, sizes, shapes and shines — like us! Each one is beautiful in its own way and appeals to a different audience — like us!

There are four main grades of diamonds with additional ratings, but let's stick to these four: cut, clarity, color and carat weight. What reflective qualities do you want to show the world, and how shiny do you want the diamonds in your movie to be?

Think of it this way: the master diamond cutter (Creator) has created the facets on the diamond to allow Light to reflect from one facet to another. The Light dances inside the stone reflecting back through its surface a multi-spectrum display of brilliant Light in a mirror-like fashion to display its beauty. A diamond cut refers to the refractive and reflective qualities of the gemstone, determining its ability to handle and disperse Light, which leads to its brilliance. The ability to absorb and reflect Light gives us the opportunity to become a mirror displaying purity in all its shining brilliance.

In our life, we determine the speed at which Light interacts with us, determining our ability to handle and reflect Light back out into the world. We have more in common with diamonds than we thought!

PURITY, MOVIE SET, GO!

Your pattern of perfection was created by the Source of all being, the pure Godhead of life. We are created in absolute perfection of purity. The qualities of love are active within us. How we use them is our choice.

In a pure state, we are electronic in nature. In the center of the atoms of our body lives an electron that is alive. Our cells vibrate to this purity, which is a place within us discord cannot enter or contaminate. Think of it as you would think of the purity of a flawless diamond. This flame of purity, electronic in nature, moves around the center of every atom of the body.

We have become atomic from discord and impurities created through free will. Our atomic consciousness must be purified before the perfection of the electronic life force can be released fully into our life and our outer activities. Restoring this purity will be our number one priority in the return to higher electronic frequencies. It also makes for one exciting movie set!

> *"All matter originates and exits only by virtue of a force which brings the particle of an atom to vibration and holds this most minute solar system of the atom together. We must assume behind this force the existence of a conscious and intelligent mind. This mind is the matrix of all matter."*
>
> — Max Planck

To the influences of our inner and outer world we give our Power to reflect onto the movie screen of our life. Being magnetic in nature, we attract good through transmuting the shadows we have created, so if you don't like what is showing up on your screen, you will need to flip the lens around. Throw illuminated Light on impurity (negativity, fear, and its family) and transform all into purity (positivity, love, and its family). This keeps the structure of our foundation strong beneath us. Hafiz, a Sufi poet who expressed his love for the Divine through his poetry, reminds us — "Fear is the cheapest room in the house. I would like to see you living in better conditions."

Physical matter is the result of frequency, so your revised movie will reflect back to you the positive changes you have made. Here is a key to the areas needing the most shift; Love, Wisdom, and Power constitute a threefold activity within our Hearts, which amplifies our frequency. When directed in a positive way, this activity increases the electronic energetic vibration of our cells. Your Heart will respond to that to which you vibrate. The power of sound, thoughts and words hold incredible power for change. The music of the higher spheres vibrates to unconditional love, light and peace.

Sacred geometry and symbols are all over the Earth — clues left for us, with information encoded with the secrets of the Universe. Unconditional love consciousness and Universal love consciousness are matter in its purest form and are what we humans, in our infinite wisdom, would benefit from aspiring to.

There are unseen powers in the Universe who love when we

radiate electronic energy and are willing to assist each of us on our movie sets. To name a few: God/Higher Self, our Higher Mental Body, Angels, and Beings of Divine Love and Light. They are all excellent to partner with and are good listeners who participate with gusto on our movie set. The best part is they are at our service when we call on them.

On an important note, we might think of asking these great beings how we can serve them in their efforts to purify ourselves and our planet, listening to the wisdom coming through. It makes sense to assist those who have assisted us for so long. Co-creation is a beautiful and wondrous activity. Whatever our intention is and wherever our attention goes, there our movie unfolds.

When we vibrate slowly, negative conditions can attach to us through magnetization, anchoring in our multi-body system and accumulating over time. It is within our conscious control to refuse to engage in activities making life unbearable. Free will gives us freedom of choice. We can change the thought creating the feeling we want to disengage from. Gotta love the power of contrast!

Having the opposite sides of positive and negative to compare, engage in, and learn from gives us the wisdom to choose, grow, and expand. Many people continue to make choices that debilitate their lives, causing them to contract rather than expand.

What stories are you telling yourself, and what is your behavior saying? This speaks volumes since we create our own reality. The power we hold over our lives is astounding. Our every thought, feeling, and action affects everything in the Universe simply because everything is energy and frequency. There can be, through choice, an ocean of purity in all our thoughts, which will manifest into one form or another. A special book in my life is *Around the Year with Emmet Fox*. In this book, Emmet Fox states:

"The body, the environment, the universe itself, is plastic to our thought; and it always reflects our sincere belief."

Plastic to our thought...something to think about!

Let's talk about this statement. We are more than this physical body, which is not the "real" you. We are a luminous energy field of pure consciousness taking form in a body. Our thoughts and beliefs manifest in the physical material world. What we think upon grows and magnifies to positive or negative outcomes. If you don't want negativity in your life, keep your attention OFF those thoughts and they will atrophy. Your feelings give Power to thought — think of it like molding plastic. Even if you believe something that is not true, it will affect you as if it is, if you place enough Power behind the thought and feeling. Life is moldable, you are moldable. By altering our perceptions intentionally, we can sculpt our life. I think of it as an infinite, limitless field of possibility.

So, you see, consciousness shapes reality for all of us, so consider a good purity polish now and then. By releasing the cells of our body, Mind, and spirit from impurities, we move one step closer to freedom, to the common spiritual bond we all share. Worth the effort and then some, wouldn't you say? Nature does this intuitively and organically — a true Source of inspiration, guidance, and love. A brilliant and intuitive teacher, the essence of God is in every living thing. Ask any tree!

PURITY — THE WHOLE PICTURE

Purity is a powerful quality freeing us from limitation, leading to unrestricted freedom and joy, enhancing every area of our lives. We can all use purity to transform our lives by cooperating with our perfected self with intent and focus. One thing we can do is practice balancing the left and right hemispheres of our brain. Each side controls different types of thinking and, although these characteristics exist on both sides of the brain, they are stronger on one side than the other. Since each half has the ability to work independently like incredibly powerful computer processors running slightly different programs, it's like I am writing to two of you!

The left hemisphere is more methodical, looks at parts of the whole picture, is better at reasoning, analytics, science, numbers and languages. Have you ever wondered why it is so challenging to meditate? The left brain may find this intentional stillness and blankness to be irrational, nonsensical, or even silly!

The right hemisphere is more feeling oriented and creative. It looks at the whole picture, is more intuitive, artistic, musical and philosophical. Yet the right hemisphere, which is the first to develop, controls the left side of the body, and the left hemisphere, which develops later, controls the right side of the body.

We use different areas of our brain to function in our daily lives. Understand your strengths, and work on your weaknesses. For example, the left hemisphere is best at memory for spoken and written words. I need work in the memory department, and I know many people feel the same way. Obviously our educational system, which places more emphasis on left-brain skills, was not my strong suit! I am excellent at face recognition but not good at remembering names. I can read extremely complicated text but am not great at reiterating what I have read or heard, even though I understand it well. I like to think of my husband, Cody, as my left brain. He excels at breaking down large amounts of information into small bits containing relevant information, conveys it beautifully, and is more whole-brain balanced, or at least that's the way it looks from my vantage point.

CREATIVE CHILD'S PLAY MOVES YOU HAPPILY FORWARD

We all have challenges in different areas of our life that could use some improvement or old habits we wish to be free of. It all starts when we're young. One of the most important aspects of any child's development and education is creativity, as it plays a significant role in the growth and maturation into adulthood. As we grow out of childhood, we creatively rework the impressions we acquired during play, using our active imaginations to construct our new reel-ality, bringing us into a joyful space in which to creatively direct and star in the movie of our life.

Think of the brain as yin/yang, masculine (Mind) and feminine (Heart), and many will agree, the feminine has been denied its undeniable and immense Power in the world. We all have masculine and feminine qualities in us having nothing to do with gender. Polishing these qualities creates balance. Choosing to ignore these qualities leads to an out-of-balance condition, something we have all experienced at one time or another.

"Be sincere in your thoughts,
Be pure in your feelings.
You will not have to run after happiness.
Happiness will run after you."

— Sri Chinmoy,
from *The Wings of Joy: Finding Your Path to Inner Peace*

Allowing your imagination, your creativity, your intention, and your desire to be open to learning and discovering keeps your brain active and stimulated. Exercise your brain. Like your body, your brain needs to stay active. Life is so much sweeter when you enjoy living in your bliss! Take your attention away from unwanted habits and replace them with new habits in support of your life. This keeps your concentration on the intended change and helps transform your life.

As we strive for purity of thought, we must also make purity of Heart a priority. The reason for this is because we must be clear about our intention before reacting to life's unexpected challenges. In stressful situations, we must think through our responses and exercise control over our emotions. We live in an increasingly interconnected, global society. It is no longer possible to hear about problems and strife in another part of the world and pretend it has no effect upon our immediate surroundings. We must be prepared to respond properly when the bonds holding our society together begin to fail and we are confronted with the outcome of negative vibrations and bad decisions. Our response to discord and strife must be grounded in Love, based upon a foundation of Wisdom and Purity of intention in both Heart and Mind.

Polish the diamond of your desire, see it in its finished perfection shining out into the world. In our perfected state, we vibrate at a higher frequency and shine with diamond brilliance. The emotional frequency waves of love are high, rapid waves, in contrast to those of fear, which are long, slow waves. In our human state, we have impurities in need of a bit of polishing. Purity is like a human polishing cloth returning us to the all "natural state" of perfection, which the original designer intended us to be in.

Visualize your movie alive in bright, living colors, every detail intact. Enjoy the panoramic screening after you create all you dream and desire. Give thankful gratitude that your needs are met and your desires fulfilled. See it as complete, conducting your life in alignment with your vision.

Purity plays a unique role in our lives and is essential to claiming the powerful discovery of our I AM Heart of Hearts. We are powerful, and by feeling the connection to our strength, Power, and perfection, we defy weakness, powerlessness, and imperfection. It's not that we are perfect, but we can strive toward being our best each day. The sleeping Soul will awaken when "directed" (remember, this is your movie set, your movie, your life) to activate life toward conscious, uplifting activities.

Stake a claim on your courageous Power, because it belongs to you. Purity of Mind comes through patience and perseverance. With this discipline comes the Power of momentum as our lives move forward in a more consistent manner conducive to our happiness.

Everyone has a different standard of purity that resonates with their life path. Set your own standard of purity by engaging with the qualities of purity important to you. Trust in yourself as you listen to your intuitive nature for guidance. Purity paves the way for the wondrous movie of your life.

DEBRA'S STORYBOARD ON PURITY

Purification is an important activity for me as I enter each day. I direct my Higher Self to take the core, cause, effect, memory and record of every space and place I have ever been or will be that is not in my highest and greatest good, to be lifted up and out of me and placed into the sacred fires of transmutation. I use the violet flames for this. A small flame can easily go out with a slight breeze, but I know there are strong flames deep within my Soul capable of purifying everything. My reasons for using violet are personal. Use what resonates with you.

I imagine everything I want to release floating up and out of me into a container of some kind — a balloon, cloud, box, or whatever I choose that day. I see the image of it being handed over to my Higher Self to be transmuted and purified. For you, this could be prayer, meditation, contemplation or any daily practice you resonate with.

I see everything purified and transmuted into love, peace, joy, abundance, health, and all that serves my life's path, filling every space of my being and world. I then see and feel the blessings here for me now. At this point, I begin to pre-pave my future path by intensely visualizing.

Next, I sit in the silence filled with gratitude for all that is here and all that is yet to come into my life. I go on about my day knowing the details are being handled as I take the appropriate action steps toward my goal. The key for me is to breathe purity and Power in throughout the day, especially when a challenge arises. This way I am able to make choices and take actions that best serve to support my life and the lives of others. I keep in Mind that when I connect to my inner Power, I become a magnet for good, and life is a blessing.

YOUR PERSONAL STORYBOARD ON PURITY

1. Upon waking in the morning, I consciously seek Purity by:

____

____

____

____

____

2. In my personal daily ritual, my conscious intention is to apply Purity to:

___

___

___

___

___

3. By aligning Mind with Spirit, I bring about positive frequencies in regard to:

___

___

___

___

___

4. In the course of my daily activities, I seek Purity of Heart and Mind in these areas of my life:

___

___

___

___

___

5. My standard of Purity is:

____

____

____

____

____

6. In Light and Love, I recognize and acknowledge the following examples of Purity principles:

____

____

____

____

____

7. I choose to increase the positive Purity frequencies in my life by:

____

____

____

____

____

#4 — TREATMENT FOR SCRIPT ON PURITY

FADE IN:

Purity and wonder are not easy to hold onto as we go out into the world at large. Sarah knows these qualities are in short order in her world but is determined to live a life exemplifying these qualities.

This did not mean being the perfect goody two shoes, but to Sarah these qualities hold a feeling of seeing the world through the eyes of a child and discovering something magical for the first time. Looking at the world with eyes of wonder fills Sarah's days.

As the years go by, Sarah becomes disillusioned with her life and the world in general. She tries not to be discouraged, but daily and with more frequency she is presented with negativity in the paper, images on television and online, people saying the world is falling apart, and all manner of information that has decidedly become unpleasant with only a modicum of positivity thrown in.

Sarah has slowly lost her ability to see the beauty and abundance in the world around her, forgetting it is always there for those who have eyes to see. Instead of surrounding herself with positive people, Sarah allows herself to get sucked into negativity quicksand like many others, feeling as though she cannot escape.

Sarah is now living her life from the outside in, allowing negative influences to keep her in fear and doubt. She believes the illusion, forgetting to look inside herself for the purity and wonder she once embraced. Sarah becomes another lost Soul, forgetting all the while the choice to live in her own self-created reality she had felt earlier in life.

FADE TO BLACK

#4 — REWRITE OF TREATMENT FOR SCRIPT ON PURITY

FADE IN:

Purity and wonder are not easy to hold onto as we go out into the world at large. Sarah knows these qualities are in short order in her world but is determined to live a life exemplifying these qualities.

This did not mean being the perfect goody two shoes, but to Sarah these qualities hold a feeling of seeing the world through the eyes of a child and discovering something magical for the first time. Looking at the world with eyes of wonder fills Sarah's days.

As the years go by, Sarah realizes if she allows herself to become disillusioned with the world, as she sees many people do, something vital inside her will die a slow death. She makes a conscious choice not to be discouraged by the daily negativity in the paper, images on television and online, people saying the world is falling apart, and all manner of information that has decidedly become unpleasant with only a modicum of positivity thrown in.

Sarah turns off the news, changes the channel from CNN to Discovery, creates strong affirmations and uses them daily to stay centered in her purity and wonderment.

Sarah no longer engages in the programming of her life and continues to view the world with wonder, all the while expressing gratitude for all life. She knows good continually crosses her path, daily creating her life with purpose and clarity, to the best of her ability. Life prospers in and around Sarah's personal life, and those who know her wonder how she does it. Go ahead, ask her — Sarah loves to encourage others!

FADE TO WHITE

REEL WRAP: THE CONCEPT OF PURITY

★ Impurity is a thief who steals the Divine vitality of your perfection.

★ Free will gives you freedom of choice. You can change the thought creating the feeling you want to disengage from.

★ Your every thought, feeling, and action affects everything in the Universe simply because everything is energy and frequency.

★ You are more than this physical body, which is not the "real" you. You are a luminous energy field of pure consciousness taking form in a body. Your thoughts and beliefs manifest in the physical, material world. What you think upon grows and magnifies to positive or negative outcomes.

★ Purity is a powerful quality that can free you from limitation, leading to unrestricted freedom and joy, enhancing every area of your life.

★ Your response to discord and strife must be grounded in Love, based upon a foundation of Wisdom, and Purity of intention in both Heart and Mind.

★ When you connect to your inner Power, you become a magnet for good, and life is a blessing.

Concept #5:
CONCENTRATED ILLUMINATION

Are You The Creative Director In Your Movie?

"Absorb yourself in each moment slowly savoring the gift of life, remembering miracles are available in every moment. Your Naturally Occurring Wonder exists NOW!"

— Debra Oakland

YOU ARE GOD IN EVERYTHING

You are God in everything. Whether you choose to manifest it is up to you. You do, after all, have free will. Nothing, not unlimited success or unending misery, is ever imposed upon you. It all is your choice. The fact remains you are more than another mammal walking around on this planet. We are much more than these bodies we place so much importance on. You are created in the image of God. God is Life, Spirit, and Light. You are Life, Spirit, and Light. These are eternal attributes, the fear of death, although not a pleasant thought, is unfounded; all that dies is the physical garment you are walking around in. The real you is translated to another dimension, another plane of reality. What happens then is subject to much speculation and postulation; but the real You never dies. Your spirit is energy, and energy doesn't dissipate. It merely changes state. It's basic physics.

It may help you to imagine yourself as concentrated illumination: a Light Being inhabiting a vehicle, which stores your collected awareness (your Soul) as you creatively direct your life. Our bodies allow us to live, move, and experience our beingness out in this particular physical world. The majority of people have learned to express who they are through the body to such an extent they believe with all their being they are the body. This is part of the illusion.

"The truth is — Everything counts.
Everything.
Everything we do and everything we say
Everything helps or hurts;
Everything adds to or
Takes away from someone else."

— Countee Cullen

We are as imageless as God. The God in you is a creator, so take command and be the creative director in this great production of your life. As a magnificent, powerful being of Light and Spirit housed in your physicality, you get to create the life you desire to live and are solely responsible for your "reel" experiences.

Life is eternal; we are eternal. Each of us is an electronic Light force of such Power and beauty traveling through the eternal expanse of the Universe, creating, directing and experiencing. Our essence makes us magical, an anomaly — unique creators interacting with life on this physical plane. Concentration plays a key role in concentrated illumination.

FOCUS YOUR LENS WITH CONCENTRATION

Concentration is required from the smallest activity to the greatest achievements in life. Without focused concentration, it is difficult to be skilled in anything. Expert filmmakers understand this. Think about the many aspects of yourself you bring into the main story of your movie and how much of this was intentional.

To live our best life, it is beneficial to keep our focused intent on one area of utmost importance at a time. This requires our attention to details. If our attention is drawn away from our desired endeavor for long enough, or is too scattered, we lose our intention and may never see the physical manifestation of our desire unfold — the energetic circuit is severed, and the energy dissipates. Some say dreamers aren't doers. I disagree. We have been discouraged from dreaming, using our imagination, and engaging the power of thought.

The 1993 movie *Rudy* is the true story of Rudy Ruettiger, a boy who wanted to play football for Notre Dame. While Rudy was working the "expected job" at the steel mill, the sudden death of his friend, Pete, changed the course of his life. Rudy began pursuing his boyhood dream of playing football for Notre Dame. Being small and having a learning disability did not discourage Rudy as he continued to set small goals, staying motivated and determined. The love of the game, the concentrated illumination he shed on his goal, and the help of many mentors along the way allowed Rudy to achieve his dream.

It is to be hoped we do not go through the loss of a loved one, like Rudy did, to change the course of our life. As they say in the movie,

"Sometimes a winner is a dreamer who just won't quit."

Imagine how his actions and persistence influenced the people around him. He changed lives and gained so much, by following his dream.

What do you want to achieve, and are you determined to take the steps to make it happen? There are mentors everywhere to cheer you on, so find people who believe in you as much as you believe in yourself.

Discouragement is a concentration vampire draining the life blood out of our dreams. Encouragement is a Concentrated Illuminated Energetic Transfusion. Ideally, we want the movie of our life to authentically represent who we are to the world. Movies featuring people passionate about what they love are interesting, creative, motivating and engaging. They draw a crowd appealing to a wide range of viewers.

CONCENTRATED ENERGY

Concentrated illumination is focused energy infused with inspired Light. Combining thought, feeling, and action in a conscious, deliberate way puts you in the director's chair with authority. Energy is active, and you can direct its activity in any way you choose.

The physical aspect of our being lives in an environment bombarding us with stimulation on a daily basis; the overwhelming majority of the energy is negatively oriented. Psycholinguistics is used in all advertising and political speeches above the local level. It is designed to produce amplification of your physical and emotional cravings and desires, producing the negative excess energy oriented toward a feeling of lack. This makes it hard to reach the state of stillness required to maintain control over your thoughts.

I keep repeating this, but we do become what we think, feel, and act upon. When you live from the inside out, you stand guard over outside suggestions not in your best interest. The subconscious is where habits are formed. Over time, positive rhythmic suggestions can change old unwanted habits into new healthier ones. The subconscious Mind is connected to the Universal Mind and uses the activity of thought to create.

If a person does not believe this powerful live active energy flows in, through, and around them, they will manifest in direct proportion to their belief. It is through the conscious Mind we make choices through many forms of reasoning. Free will gives us the capability to direct the subconscious Mind. The goal is to do this in a responsible and healthy manner. You can be skeptical, that's good. Investigate the subject of energy. Look up scientific evidence.

Physics tells us a theory that all matter vibrates and has a wave component, this indicates everything is connected. We are part of a big wave of energy, all interconnected, and science is starting to document our individuality, as well. Just as every person has a unique physical fingerprint and a unique retina pattern, so do we appear to have a unique energy signature.

All of our individual energy force fields share the same Source. When simply combined, they are not just the sum of the parts; the positive and the negative energies seek balance. When combined in unity of purpose and same orientation of intention, the combined energy force field is exponentially more powerful than the larger collective sums of the individual. This is the lesson from *It's a Wonderful Life.* When George Bailey was in trouble, all the people in the community of Bedford Falls whose lives had been forever positively impacted by George's conscious choices rallied together in a united and focused intention. A miracle occurred. The focus of our attention affects our intention and determines how our personal lives play out. On a much larger scale, our collective concentrated attention plays out in the same way. The bigger picture!

When you stand as sentinel over your subconscious Mind, directing your life movie, the real fun begins by indulging your JOY! How about some spiritual sunbathing on your breaks between takes? Is your goal to live a joyful, healthy, happy, abundant life?

Of course it is! The subconscious accepts what the conscious Mind feeds it. Make sure what you are feeding it is nourishing.

Love, hope, joy, peace and unity are beneficial to the seeds we plant, feed, and water on our movie set. From our personal life to the larger moving picture, concentration is required. Our thoughts and how we direct them do matter, on so many levels. Concentrated illumination gives our dreams wings.

THE POWER OF REEL THOUGHT

> *"Every man is where he is by the law of his being; the thoughts which he has built into his character have brought him there, and in the arrangement of his life there is no element of chance, but all is the result of a law which cannot err."*
>
> — James Allen
> in *As a Man Thinketh*

We are the product of our thoughts. Without our bodies, how do we communicate? Through thought or by telepathy. Imagine transmitting thought waves out and someone who is tuned in receives them. We send and receive thoughts daily. How many times have you found yourself thinking about someone and they call you? This is not chance or serendipity. We are often not aware of it, but it is how we pray, meditate, and use faith; by tuning in to the God of our knowing, and in turn, the Universe attempts to give us what we need at any particular time in order to answer those prayers or meditations.

How do ideas fly into our thoughts? We can pick up their vibrations while in a receptive, creative mode. Think of a great idea someone abandoned right at conception. You pick it up from an energy wave resonating with your intention, and all of a sudden this idea is given new life through you. This is why an idea cannot be patented or copyrighted. The idea is only the seed and the seed must be cultivated and grown before it can be distinguished from any other seed. Most people give up on their dream just as they are ready to receive their greatest desire. Hopping from one thing to the next in search of the dream, or playing small, does not yield the desired harvest.

This all comes down to everything moving energetically through time and space. Some people are more sensitive and consciously aware of the energy around them, but everyone has intuitive abilities. Since childhood, I have been sensitive to the energy around me. These feelings or intuition I receive about locations or people have served me well throughout my life. I trust my inner higher guidance to steer me in the right direction. Even if it creates a challenging experience from which I need to learn or grow, I know it is for my highest and greatest good. In hindsight, what may not have made sense at the time I was going through the experience served to provide wisdom for something later in my journey.

Trust your inner guidance; it is there to assist you. Deep Soul communication gives us the ability to transfer thought into the different forms of manifestation we desire. It can be easy to forget we are more than our bodies. This immense, expansive, and beautiful

Soul we are experiences all the varied aspects of life by using the body within which to navigate.

TAKE BACK YOUR DIRECTORIAL POWER — IT BELONGS TO YOU!

There is possibility in anything and everything. If your life is not working out as you would like, ask yourself some questions. Are you taking command as the lead director in your movie? How is the clarity when you look through the camera lens? Do you need to revise your script, set up auditions, design and build a new set, or kick the negative critics off the set? Are you enjoying the clips you are currently able to view? Life is ever changing, as is your movie, so there is always some editing to be attended to. The life of a movie director is a busy one, so remember to take care of your physical, mental and spiritual health each day.

What creates the world as we see it? Everything we see began first as thought. Personal development literature talks about thoughts creating reality. Most thoughts are random as we go about our day, without our conscious control exercised over many of them. We worry about the day-to-day details. We think about our family and friends. We entertain our dreams, our goals, and our desires. We wonder about how we are perceived by others. We choose which of these thoughts we are going to focus on and germinate.

Thoughts, whether given over to love and light or thrown into the negative swamp of fear, will manifest themselves regardless. This is simply because your subconscious Mind accepts what you feed it without question, and is why it is important to stay positive and keep your guard up. It is not easy, but with consistent practice you will become an excellent director of positivity!

Throughout time people have written and spoken about the power of thought, using it successfully in their own lives. Many are familiar with the research of the late Dr. Masaru Emoto on water. In his book *The Hidden Messages in Water* and books to follow, Dr. Emoto discusses and shows us that water exposed to negativity can form distorted shapes in shattered formations when frozen. Positive exposure can create beautiful crystal snowflake formations. After freezing, the aesthetics of the resulting crystals are then examined with microscopic photography. He tells us thought energy can affect the physical properties of matter, such as music, prayer, concentrated thought or words on paper.

Having met Dr. Emoto twice at lectures, I am a big fan! His research on water crystals on his website and in his books show the power positive or negative thoughts and words can create. I find value in writing the word 'love' or 'perfect health' on paper and putting it under food or liquids. Write anything you like and have fun experimenting with it.

Few people are capable of exercising complete control over their thoughts. The ones who are able to exercise this kind of control hold great power and are able to manifest their desires for positive or negative outcomes. Studies in quantum physics and quantum mechanics show not only is a there a connection between the mind and physical matter, which endeavors to explain much that has been previously unexplained, but also, our observation of reality, changes reality.

There are many uncertainties between energy, time, and space. The simple things are often hidden in plain sight. Universal Laws and Principles are a perfect example. When we are ready to tune into these principles and put them into daily practice, dreams will begin to come alive before us. When we learn to walk in Light and Love, we see things others cannot and our vision begins to manifest in our reality.

What if we preset a specific time for this "light" to go on in the cells of our bodies, for reasons unbeknownst to us at this time? Did we put clues upon the trail of life experience to jog our memory at just the right time, waking us up to our immense power? When the light comes on, it is concentrated illumination, a personal sacred journey for each individual.

> *"Our deepest fear is not that we are inadequate. Our deepest fear is that we are powerful beyond measure. It is our light, not our darkness that most frightens us. We ask ourselves, Who am I to be brilliant, gorgeous, talented, fabulous? Actually, who are you not to be? You are a child of God. Your playing small does not serve the world. There's nothing enlightened about shrinking so that other people won't feel insecure around you. We are all meant to shine, as children do. We were born to make manifest the glory of God that is within us. It's not just in some of us; it's in everyone.*

> *And as we let our own light shine, we unconsciously give other people permission to do the same. As we're liberated from our own fear, our presence automatically liberates others."*
>
> — Marianne Williamson
> in *A Return To Love*

Giving your power away to create change in your life is not a pleasant thought, is it? We give our power away through disconnecting from Source; but Source did not go anywhere. The Universe is, was, and always will be. Reconnection is a thought away. Moving from darkness into Light is as simple as flipping the switch that reorients our intention.

I like to think of thought as an important element in concentrated illumination — our focused thought being the gateway to our powerful Perfected Presence, The Universal Mind. Even in the awareness we are in the presence of our own greatness, much of the time we forget who we are and the power at our disposal.

Through concentrated illumination, this energy infused with Light guides us perfectly. The power of living in Light and Love is never angry, bitter, vengeful or controlling. This power is loving, peaceful, allowing, creative and balanced. If you have fallen out of balanced harmony in some important areas of your life do not despair. Click on the concentrated illumination switch and take back your directorial power — It belongs to you.

POWER, POWER, ON THE WALL

There is an electrical current within our bodies which originates from Source and is polarized toward our Higher Perfected Self. We are, at our fundamental manifestation, pure energy, this is how we can have confidence in knowing we are eternal and one with Source. Energy never dissipates; it merely transforms into another manifestation. Our energetic force field extends out from our bodies for some distance. When our harmonious current of Power is interrupted or stopped, little of our "good" can get through, if any at all. The flow gets a kink, stopped up by engaging with the forces of fear and negativity, or as I like to call them, "the critics." Choosing to think, feel, and respond with Love restores the flow.

Where have you allowed the flow of harmony in certain areas of your life to be interrupted? Go easy on yourself; we all have areas in need of improvement. Look at the lessons learned and the wisdom gained that can be implemented into your daily life. Recognizing old patterns and eliminating them changes your movie script, which in turn, changes your life.

Your "Individualized Personal Power" is not in a family member, a friend, or a stranger. It's in you. This is your movie, not theirs. If you wish to believe otherwise, you can go on living from the outside looking in until you are ready for a shift. To direct your movie creatively as you see fit, take back your Power from wherever it has been. Connect with your confidence, courage, and enthusiastic creativity. Living in Light and Love is delicious, addicting, and good for you.

Our Higher Perfected Self loves to communicate with us and touch our lives in miraculous ways. We have a direct line by consciously directing our attention with focused intention to this inner Source of Power. Remember, thought is energy, as is all life. Your thoughts, which I trust you create from a space of love, can energetically bring the unformed into form. Applying the natural laws governing the Universe is creation, and the right use of free will.

When the flow of your desire is disturbed by non-harmonious thoughts and activities, there will be an interruption of your good. There is minimal connection to your infinite Power if you are not in tune with it or if the circuit is cut off or unformed. Similar to folding a water hose in half or by stepping on it, the flow is cut off. Unfolding or stepping off the hose is the obvious solution to unimpeded flow. I remind myself, when needed, to step off the hose! Complying with Universal Laws and Principles, allows our Higher Self to do its work through us unimpeded.

As we hold our peace, our Higher Self/Inner Power Source will handle the details, seen and unseen. It is only a question of time before the manifestation shows up, if you stay focused and true to your intention. Silence the inner critic, keep your attention on your excellent movie-making skills, carry on in joyful creativity, and watch the excellent movie reviews come pouring in.

THE CONCENTRATED ILLUMINATION OF FEELING

On an emotional level, we "feel." What we think about with focused intensity and constancy (concentrated illumination) engages the feelings, which then connect to unseen magnetic forces. If we don't like the direction our life is taking, we can opt for a different direction simply by choosing a different scenario. We are as limitless as our choices. Have you noticed nothing in the world changes except the supporting actors, the costumes, the makeup and the location or set? We are the writers, producers, directors, lead actors, editors and so much more — of our individual life productions.

What do you want the title of your movie to be? Here is a list of imaginary movie titles that could be coming to your Mind Metroplex very soon:

Be Careful What You Don't Wish For — A horror movie in which a woman trades her dreams for the illusion of security and ends up living a nightmare.

You Get What You Give — A romantic comedy showing what happens when two people try to outdo each other with random acts of kindness and end up falling in love.

The War of the Egos — An apocalyptic vision of the destructive forces unleashed when blind ambition clashes with selfish motives in a quest for money and power.

Games Afoot — A science fiction thriller about a woman who does something about social programming gone badly.

The Joyful Journey of Max Transformation — A wonderful little independent film about a man who finds heaven on Earth when he chooses to positively impact the world around him.

You can make up your own titles, but you get the picture!

Become a master at creating a purpose-driven life of joy. Experience is the best teacher. Let's all pay more attention to what is showing up in our movies. As Nora Ephron pointed out, "Above all, be the heroine of your life, not the victim."

We can talk about concentrated illumination and creating the life we want, but until we experience moments of joy, peace, and love flowing in, through, and out of us to any degree, we are only conceptualizing the ideal. We need experiential evidence of our own.

In a detached fashion, be present to observe. Realize we are creating it all. Every person, situation, and event occurring in our lives was choreographed by each of us for our energetic and vibrational growth. From a nonjudgmental mindset, witness what is unfolding in your daily life. As a creator, the only power any experience has over us is the power we give it and our judgments of it. The collective experience is not mine or yours alone. We are all going through this together. Your personal quest belongs exclusively to you. People will continue evolving on a road of individual self-realization as they ascend into dimensions of higher frequency.

Selfishness and greed have destroyed some of the greatest civilizations on Earth. Now is the time to be masters over ourselves and our world! Let's design the future with purpose, vision, unity and love, become responsible stewards and co-creators working together. If not us, then who? If not now, when? It is time to take a stand for the God in each of us, the life in each of us. The God and Life in you is the God and Life in me. Let's pause for a small intermission and an exercise in stillness.

AN EXERCISE IN STILLNESS

The best way to experience this state of awareness is to stop all activity and imagine yourself simply and purely as thought.

Sit or lie comfortably in stillness.

Allow yourself to feel weightless.

Pretend for a few minutes you have no body.

Let the thoughts float in and out until the noises around you fade into the background.

Consciously begin directing your thoughts for a few minutes in a profound and powerful way. Your thoughts have no limitation, so enjoy the feeling of freedom as you define the details.

Allow your imagination to bring all you desire onto the panoramic movie screen of your life. Even if present circumstances make it seem as if these dreams and desires could never be a reality in your life, give yourself permission to play along and have fun with the experience. Repeat aloud to yourself.

"I give myself permission to believe I am worthy.

I allow myself to believe anything is possible."

Go for it. Imagine anything; no matter how crazy it seems. No one knows what you are visualizing. You won't be judged for it. This is your time. Dare to visualize your ideal life. Use all your senses. Make it as real as the world you see when you open your eyes. Hear it. Touch it. Smell it. Taste it. Arrange your vision the way you see it in your Heart and Mind.

Now, pick ONE thing to concentrate on. How does it feel, even if you think of it as a fantasy? Allow yourself to sink into it. If you find random thoughts coming in to interrupt your fun zone, let the thoughts pass and refocus. Be in this space as long as you like. When you reach a point of simply being with this one desire upon which you have focused your attention, express gratitude. Then get up and go about your day.

Continue practicing each day until you master control of your conscious thought on this ONE desire. You are directing your subconscious and reprogramming the cells of your body to respond. This response can motivate and align you with people, places, and things drawing your desire toward you in the form you are ready to manifest. You will grow stronger, and your life will begin to change, because you are mastering you. I used this a great deal while writing the book you are now reading.

> *"All things are created twice. There's a mental or first creation, and a physical or second creation to all things. The physical creation follows the mental, just as a building follows a blueprint. If you don't make a conscious effort to visualize who you are and what you want in life, then you empower other people and circumstances to shape you and your life by default."*
>
> — Stephen R. Covey
> *The 7 Habits of Highly Effective People*

We are thought in its purest form, and as directors, naturally we want our movie to be the best quality it can be. Start with one desire, because this concentrates the focused activity and illuminates it. Yes, concentrated illumination! Now, as you add feeling to this desire, taking action without resistance, you are on the road to success. Time to let go and allow God/Goddess to fully express in, through, and out from you.

Without the body, our Soul knows exactly what to do. It has functioned this way since the beginning of time and will continue to do so. Do you ever wonder why we have been conditioned to overlook the extreme benefits of the power of thought? This has affected us individually and collectively. The outer world and its influences can seem to hold more "reel" power, but it is not so. Your Power lives in you.

Why not be actively involved in a bigger plan as you ascend into higher frequencies, headed to new and even greater adventures? Learning to consciously control your thoughts is your right. It's exciting to contemplate, practice, and experience this movie-making magic!

We get caught up in what the outer world endlessly offers, and it never seems to be enough, because we are missing the ability to use a key part of ourselves we are chasing after. Are you open to the possibility or probability your thoughts have immense power to assist you in creating your reality? Thoughts combined with feeling and action put you in the director seat with authority. Yes, it does! Changing your movie will change your life.

CONCENTRATED CREATIVITY

Creativity is one of the many unlimited powers we have been granted at birth. Getting in line with our creativity as a concentrated activity helps us express authentically from our core, where the fire of spirit is alive with passion. This leads to enthusiasm in action, setting into motion the desire to manifest our creation in physical form. While all this is happening, there is an energetic circuitry flowing freely as we are in high gear creatively. It makes us feel alive and vital to be creating at our best.

When we are not in line with our creativity, we break the circuit, losing part of our vital life force. Listening to "the critics" increases the static, tunes us out, and disrupts the creative flow. This interruption can come from many sources outside ourselves, convincing us what we are creating is not good enough, causing us to feel less than, uninspired, frustrated or depressed. Trying to get on track can be hit or miss.

Think about how it feels when you are fired up with creative excitement. You are tuned in, tapped in, and turned on to your creative frequency, and the static is tuned out. It's called being in the flow, and what a wonderful place it is! Your channel is clear, and what you seek is seeking you. Your hearts desires gravitate toward you in perfect harmony.

What happens when you meet resistance? Some people fold up like an old lawn chair and quit. Others grab the reins tighter and press on through toward the goal. It is entirely up to you as to which of these people you will choose to be. Success is not easy. It takes hard work and perseverance to hone raw talent into craftsmanship. It takes moxie to start with a blank page and see the vision through from story to book to blockbuster movie.

Stephen King is known for having more book adaptations (film, television series, mini-series and comic books) than any other living author. His estimated net worth is $400 million and his books have sold more than 350 million copies. Success did not come easy...

Carrie was the first of many great movies based upon his work, but it almost never happened. In 1972, King received over 30 rejections on the manuscript and threw it into the trash. His wife, Tabitha, pulled it out, read it, and encouraged him to send it out one more time. In January of 1973, he submitted the manuscript to Doubleday and they gave him a $2,500 advance. The following month, they sold the paperback rights for $400,000. Stephen King has became a wildly successful literary icon.

By giving ourselves permission to create with uninterrupted harmony, we are saying yes to life, and as we do, life says yes to us. Staying in the flow, as one project or desire is creatively fulfilled, builds momentum and assists us in moving on to create in even more extraordinary ways.

Surround yourself with supportive people who have a good sense of self-worth. We all benefit from cheerleaders in our life who are positive and motivated themselves. As movie directors, we can all use some behind the scenes support! Build a strong relationship with yourself and with those who support and inspire you. Internal validation builds a level of confidence that is unshakable.

Think about people who are creative in the extreme. Many of them have been ridiculed, denied, and lived through many challenges to achieve their goal. These people have one thing in common: they did not give up; they stayed the course, true to the dream. Some have gone on to become icons, revered for their passionate creativity and perseverance.

Your creative Power is as unlimited as you are, and simply by setting it into motion, life expands in a joyous way. Find what sparks your core of creativity and connect with it as you ride the wave all the way to completion. Master your destiny through your own creative Power wanting to express through you. You carry a gift unique only to you. Allow the world to enjoy YOU in all you choose to create.

Our life or "Light" essence contains the Power of the Universe. This Power flows from Source into our Higher Perfected Self, into our Heart, which then animates our world. How you "Power Up" is your choice. The Light essence you are, in all its perfection, contains within it everything you require. Yet there we go looking everywhere outside of ourselves, searching, constantly searching.

In the Herman Hesse novel, *Siddhartha*, Siddhartha and his companion, Govinda, set out in search of enlightenment, which leads Siddhartha to the conclusion that the outer world is a distraction, and inner personal experience is shown to be the best way to approach the understanding of reality on the road to enlightenment. Experiencing ourselves creatively is one of the keys that opens the door to our concentrated illumination, which is enlightening. When we go out searching for what we already are, finding what we are not, we will be directed back inside where the storehouse of our inner knowing lives.

VISION IS POWER

> *"When we try to make everything clear, we make everything confused. If, however, we admit one mysterious thing in the Universe, then everything else becomes clear in the Light of that. The sun is so bright, so mysterious, that one cannot look at it, and yet in the Light of the sun everything else is seen."*
>
> — Fulton J. Sheen

Vision, creativity, and passion carry us to places we did not know it was possible to go. How do we learn to believe in ourselves so much that we dispel fear and doubt? This is a question I ask myself often. Intellectually, I know it is found through opening doors to new experiences and living life courageously. Spiritually, I know it is from staying connected to my Higher Self, Heart-centered and Divinely guided.

Many people have lived a lifetime of being told they are not good enough, smart enough, or capable enough. All manner of constraints and dictates try to define and regulate us in the outer world. How long are you going to buy into the opinions of naysayers? Sometimes the biggest naysayer is your own self-doubt!

As you fill up with hope, confidence, determination, go out and give others the encouragement you would want someone to give you. Being comfortable makes us feel safe, but in the long run...

> *"A comfort zone is a beautiful place, but nothing ever grows there."*
>
> — Author Unknown

I like my comfort zone, thank you very much, but as the years roll by, I know what creates growth is change, and this means leaving the cozy comfort zone behind from time to time. Often we are like children, holding on to our "blankey" with a thumb in our mouth, trailing our blanket of comfort behind. One part of the process of becoming an adult requires we leave the security blanket behind and move forward, embracing change.

To grow into spiritual adulthood, afford yourself the clarity to see your vision for the future, silence the critics, and connect daily to your God Source of all good. The obstacles clouding your vision will clear.

A simple quote by Sri Aurobindo says it perfectly:

> *"In order to see, you have to stop being in the middle of the picture."*

Getting out of our own way is not easy, but it is well worth the repeated effort. Spend as much time as possible envisioning the life you want to live. Examine what is truly important for your vision to succeed. What is the motivation behind the vision, and how do you see it unfolding? Your vision is powerful, and when you use it wisely with a loving Heart, it will be a blessing in all areas of your life.

As an exercise, write the eulogy scene for your own funeral. What music would be played? Who would attend? What would they say about you? How would your life be remembered? Make it as detailed as you can.

BE A LIVING DIRECTOR OF CONCENTRATED ILLUMINATION

There seems to be a sense of uneasiness in many people, no matter who they are, where they live, or their station in life. Until we each learn to hold the vision of love for ourselves and others, there will be dark clouds in the way.

Transcending separation is about directing each other back to our individualized concentrated illumination which powers us up for unconditional love. Many people have lost the connection to their inner Light. Part of the disconnect comes from expecting the outer world to fill all our needs. As mentioned repeatedly, the answers we search for are on the inside, where the Light is ready and waiting to be switched on. It may be on a dimmer switch, but you control the switch!

Trust in yourself to control what happens in you, not to you. Learn to apply the Universal Laws and Principles of Life. They are unchangeable, constant, and ever-present for our use. When we learn to draw into our life what we need, when we need it, people take notice. We become a way-shower to others who want to live in their own self-created reality of peace and joy.

You, as the peace-commanding presence, no longer feel a need to react to triggers that fired you up, causing conflict. If you have an issue that comes up and needs to be resolved, respond rather than react. Give yourself time to make an insightful decision. You now become the non-reactive observer witnessing the unfolding movie you intentionally wrote and directed. Replacing those old triggers with authority and using your inner Power to direct your outer life, gives your movie a whole new perspective!

You may notice family and friends who spend time around you will gain a new level of appreciation and awareness. It matters not if they hold the same beliefs; know your peaceful presence of Love and Light can touch their lives in wondrous ways.

It's good to spend time with people we genuinely like, as well as people who embody the great qualities of life we personally admire and aspire to. Take the time to write down the names of people who inspire greatness in others. Actions speak louder and with more clarity than any words. How often have you heard the old adage, "Watch what people do, not what they say"? Listen to the messages people are sending when they speak. Whose footsteps are you following and why? It's in our best interest to look to those who live their best life, because they encourage us to do the same.

Films do this in subtle, entertaining ways. Take a look at a few films that were box office hits that in my opinion share deeply significant messages. A great example is the 1993 classic *Groundhog Day*, starring Bill Murray. In the film, selfish and cynical Pittsburgh television weatherman, Phil Connors (Murray), wakes to find himself doomed to repeat the same tedious day over and over again until he learns to become a better person. What is the message? We only have one moment in which to live: the present. We must live it to its fullest.

Then there's the 1983, Bruce Beresford-directed film, *Tender Mercies,* about a broken-down, alcoholic country singer named Mac Sledge who finds enough love and redemption in the middle of East Texas to resume his career and take back control of his life. Robert Duvall won the Best Actor Oscar for his portrayal of Sledge. This beautifully tender yet powerful film was written by Horton Foote. The message is to never give up on yourself, because Love will find you and Love will forgive you of your past transgressions.

Then there's *Contact*. This 1997 masterpiece film adaptation of Carl Sagan's book by the same name features Jodi Foster as brilliant and driven astrophysicist, Ellie Arroway, who only believes in science. She has spent her entire career seeking proof of extraterrestrial life. While Ellie is at the Arecibo radio telescope Observatory, she meets her spiritual counterpart, Palmer Joss, played by Matthew McConaughey. Their brief but intense relationship takes a back seat when Ellie picks up a definite signal from an intelligent Source near the star, Vega. The Mind-bending twists and turns that ensue show us the full gamut of human intellect and emotion, good and bad.

The message is truth, no matter how we as humans try to package it, market it, or manipulate it. In the end, truth will prevail and Love will find a way.

We are helping to birth a new reality, a New Earth, as we raise our individual energetic vibrational frequency to heightened levels. Our energetic blueprint will shift as this journey progresses. A strong foundation will determine the stability in our lives; a weak foundation will crumble beneath our feet. Universal Laws and Principles provide us with a solid foundation of building blocks with which to build our structure.

The conflicting messages out in the world will drift farther and farther away, as they will hold little credence. We will find ourselves living in the world, but no longer of it. There will be no need to convince anyone we are doing the right thing, because we will be living from the inside out authentically.

How can our Higher Self assist us for "optimum" results without getting our attention and cooperation? It can't. If there is something in our life needing a resolution, we need to pay attention to the clues leading us to new awareness. By taking responsibility for creating the challenge, we can release its hold on us, which moves us to a new level of concentrated illumination.

YOUR SET DESIGN

Your movie set needs a beautiful nature setting, and since this is sacred territory, you design it the way you love to experience nature. You plant seeds of harmony on the set, water them with Love, and allow the sunlight of your Heart (concentrated energy infused with Light) and the Power of your attention to shine on them. Nature is where people go when seeking peace, rest, and moments of respite from the world, and just what you need for some of the scenes in your movie.

There is a good chance many of the people on your movie set enjoy the same nature scenarios as you. Nature understands abundance and is a way-shower for us. She deserves our utmost care, respect, and gratitude. We humans constantly get distracted, so concentration is a tool that teaches us mastery over the world of form and builds momentum as we hone our skills. Do you think Mother Nature is distracted when creating? No, her whole energy is focused on the creation at hand. Without a word being spoken, nature knows what to do instinctively. Nature is perfect for any movie set, beautifully conveying nature's living theater, teaching us and providing visuals that delight and amaze us in their timeless perfection.

DEBRA'S STORYBOARD ON CONCENTRATED ILLUMINATION

I sit in the quiet stillness of my sacred space, calling in a beautiful luminous white Light, which I think of as concentrated illumination. I see myself completely immersed in this pillar of Light, feeling protected and safe. As I continue to meditate, pray, and listen, I feel lighter as the cares of the world slip away. My imagination begins playfully creating scenes I can place and direct in the movie of my life. I mentally and visually pre-pave the dreams and desires important to me, and I then see and feel them as complete.

As I go about my day, I feel good, knowing this illuminated Light is helping to guide my way through each moment. During the day, I continue to visualize this tube of Light in and all around me. In this space, one important step for me is to see the world as whole, not broken, illumined in this healing Light. People are happy, at peace, and supporting each other, while living in Unity and Oneness with each other and our Earth. Our connection to our perfection binds us together. It is a beautiful experience.

It is important to protect your mental, physical, and emotional energetic fields with white Light each day before you step out into the world. It's like a refreshing shower of Light.

YOUR PERSONAL STORYBOARD ON CONCENTRATED ILLUMINATION

1. Upon awakening, I consciously shine my Light, with focused intent, upon:

____

____

____

____

____

2. In my personal daily spiritual ritual, I feel infused with Light, to prepare for:

____

____

____

____

____

3. By aligning Mind with Spirit, I recognize I will have Concentrated Illumination regarding:

____

____

____

____

____

4. In my daily walk, I shall be a vibratory match to what I want to experience in my life, like:

____

____

____

____

____

5. I can freely become a witness, using Love and Light to respond to:

____

____

____

____

____

6. In Light and Love, I recognize and acknowledge these principles operating in my life:

____

____

____

____

____

7. The situations I choose to change with Concentrated Illumination are:

____

____

____

____

____

#5 — TREATMENT FOR SCRIPT ON CONCENTRATED ILLUMINATION

FADE IN:

Quinn is an artist at Heart. The colors of the rainbow flow through him like liquid energy looking for an outlet on canvas. Brave and bold, he paints, inspired by all he views in life.

As Quinn loses himself with abandon in his chosen art form, each day passes by in a state of peace and happiness. Art fulfills him, but others do not seem to feel the love and energy he imparts into his work, his passion. Over time, the lack of art sales brought him to the realization he had chosen an impractical life to pay his bills. Quinn gives up on his dream and takes a job related to his college degree.

Life as a stock broker leaves Quinn feeling empty. He is no longer creating or living his passion. He works in a large open office space filled with cubicles under fluorescent lights and surrounded by hectic but less than fulfilling activity. He spends his day on the telephone and staring at a computer screen to keep track of his clients' investments. Quinn's waking hours become an endless stream of transaction reports to clients. Drinking has become a welcome friend to distract him from the long days at work.

Sidetracked by the trappings of life, his wings are clipped as he steps inside the cage, never knowing the door is still open. He dreams of a successful art career but never has the courage to believe in himself and his God-given talent. Over the years, going from job to job to support himself, Quinn never finds the time to connect with the one thing that brings him joy or with the belief art could be his life.

FADE TO BLACK

#5 — REWRITE OF TREATMENT FOR SCRIPT ON CONCENTRATED ILLUMINATION

FADE IN:

Quinn is an artist at Heart. The colors of the rainbow flow through him like liquid energy looking for an outlet on canvas. Brave and bold, he paints, inspired by all he views in life.

As Quinn loses himself with abandon in his chosen art form, each day passes by in a state of peace and happiness. Art fulfills him, but others do not seem to feel the love and energy he imparts into his work, his passion. Confident they will, he presses on. Quinn refuses to give up his dream of being a fulltime artist. He daily visualizes the art he wishes to create, as well as consistent and abundant sales. Giving up what he most loves in life never occurs to him.

Quinn ponders how to make money and continue selling art, and soon finds a job at an art gallery, connecting with other artists, understanding the importance of keeping the flow of energy directed toward his passion in art. This provides an avenue for inspiration, creativity, and success.

Through Quinn's contacts in the art world, he is now able to show his art in multiple venues. Having built a credible name in the art world, Quinn's goal is to begin teaching art to children. He has given his life to his passion, understanding the many possibilities have grown into probabilities. Quinn not only teaches children art, but the importance of individuality, confidence, self-love and appreciation for all life.

"The secret of happiness is expressing one's full potential and bringing joy to others," he tells them. "Never be afraid to reach for the stars! People around the world embrace art, enjoying the passionate creativity of the artist."

FADE TO WHITE

REEL WRAP: THE CONCEPT OF CONCENTRATED ILLUMINATION

★ The God in you is a creator. Take command, and be the creative director in the great production of your life.

★ Be open to the possibility or probability that your thoughts have immense power to assist you in creating your reality. Thoughts combined with feeling and action put you in the director seat with authority. Changing your movie will change your life!

★ Your life or "Light" essence contains the Power of the Universe. This Power flows from Source into your Higher Perfected Self, into your Heart, which then animates your world. Power Up each day, and give birth to something wonderful.

★ Take a stand for the God in you, the Life in each of us. The God and Life in you is the God and Life in me.

★ Trust in yourself to control what happens in you, not to you.

★ Listen to the messages people are sending when they speak. Whose footsteps are you following and why?

★ With a challenge of any kind, pay attention to the clues leading you to new awareness. Some of the greatest contributions on Earth have come from the greatest challenges people have endured.

Concept #6: PEACE

Who's Going to Make the First Move?

"I AM blessed in peace and harmony. I AM a fascinating symphony."

— Debra Oakland

PEACE IS OUR ACTION HERO

Peace is not weak or powerless, and neither are you. Choosing peace taps you directly into your inner Power station. Peace is our action hero, a concentrated activity bringing harmony into every space it occupies. We all have a favorite action hero (male or female) who faces threats in unique ways, taking courageous action. They confront fear face to face and never stop until peace prevails! Our action heroes find solutions and translate them into action.

It takes the power of our attention to hold peace in a world less than peaceful. Peace is active, and if we wish to have it, we must participate with it. Find the action hero living in you. An advantage on any movie set!

Everyone has experienced situations with family members, friends, or people we work with on our movie set who have presented us with a challenge. It takes inner control to remain peaceful, to respond, rather than react, yet that's what conscious movie directors do. Reacting and responding are birds of a different feather. Reacting gives us no time; responding gives us time to peacefully choose a non-reactive direction. Peace is the best option, yet the need to be heard or defend ourselves is second nature.

If you feel like reacting, ask yourself, "What is triggering this reaction inside me?" Have you heard the saying, "What you resist persists"? The more we fight against someone or something, the slower we move forward toward a peaceful resolution. Be responsible for your reactions and actions. If you have created a difficulty, find a workable solution that targets peace and brings mutual harmony to the table. If time allows, I have personally found waiting three days before responding is golden! This allows everyone to cool their jets, giving all parties involved an opportunity to gain a new level of perspective, providing the best outcome.

In the presence of someone speaking discordantly, try mentally repeating, "I choose peace" as they are talking. Use an image, thought, or words to keep you calm, holding the feeling as you listen to the message they are conveying. When a conversation is heading in a negative direction, throw in a positive response or two. As you rewrite the script on demand, notice how the flow changes!

Choosing peace as we hand any situation over to our Higher Self is where miracles can and do happen. There are seen and unseen forces at work for us, and as we hold our undisturbed peace, Universal Intelligence is given the chance to handle the details in ways we are not aware of. It's like hitting the reset button.

Being in control of our thoughts and feelings, rather than controlled by them, keeps stress and anxiety levels low and vibrational frequencies high. Imagine how people feel when others have an agenda to take their power away by controlling them. This causes resentment and lowers vibrational frequencies for all involved. Giving our power away simply does not feel good. Even though some will allow it, the higher road is to honor people with kindness, understanding, and peaceful respect.

> *"Stillness in the winds of chaos is a mighty sword."*
> — Debra Oakland

PEACEFUL WARRIOR

Remaining peaceful with positive awareness assists our energy fields to vibrate at a higher level. In the 2006 movie *Peaceful Warrior*, Dan Millman is a college gymnast who had it all, including a shot at the Olympics. He was hit by a car and told he might never walk again. Nick Nolte plays the wise Socrates, who continues to question every assumption in Dan's life.

Sting, British musician and singer-songwriter, praised this film, saying:

> *Peaceful Warrior is an important film, an inspiring film, and a film that could change lives."*

Phil Jackson, Coach of the Los Angeles Lakers, had this to say:

> *"Peaceful Warrior is a movie that captures what I strive to do to gain peak performance from the players. The movie goes right to the essence — Zensational!!"*

Tony Robbins, Author and motivational speaker, was just as effusive with his praise:

> *"See this film and it will impact the course of your life forever."*

Deepak Chopra, Author of *Peace Is the Way*, declared:

> *"Peaceful Warrior challenges you to go beyond ego-based success and understand that the way to fulfillment is through higher consciousness."*

Eckhart Tolle, Author of *The Power of Now*, said:

> *"A stunning and extraordinary film that takes you on a journey out of your mind and into the present moment. Watch it and be transformed."*

The plot and characters touch the Soul on a deep level. I feel this is a movie to draw strength from for so many reasons, but most of all, because a young man finds peace in his darkest hours. Dan Millman has continued to write, speak, and encourage people worldwide. In his book, *Way of the Peaceful Warrior: A Book That Changes Lives,* he wrote:

> *"There is no need to search; achievement leads to nowhere. It makes no difference at all, so just be happy now! Love is the only reality of the world, because it is all One, you see.... There is no way to peace; peace is the way. There is no way to love; love is the way."*
>
> — Dan Millman

Bypassing the Ego to find the true importance and meaning driving our Soul prepares our wings for flight. Part of the superhero growth process is choosing to handle challenges in peace, never allowing an outer source to hold power over the outcome. Opportunities show up when we have the courage to face difficulties on higher ground. As a "Peaceful Warrior," you are the miracle. Each moment is the only one that matters. Look for the lesson. Ask how you can learn, grow, and prosper from it. Peace is strength in action, and you will grow stronger from participating with it.

APPRECIATION & GRATITUDE

Have you ever gone to great lengths for someone just to bring a smile to their face or to encourage them in some way that would bring them more peace, yet you felt the gesture was not appreciated? We've all been there but are often not aware of the level of gratitude the person truly felt or how a smile or gesture of kindness affected them. You could have influenced their life so much that they took action, and rewrote bits of their personal script, which then changed their movie, changing the course of their life.

A ten-minute independent film, *Change for a Dollar,* written, directed, and produced by Sharon Wright, is a perfect example of this. It is a delightful film about a homeless man and the Power of one dollar. Sharon Wright asks us, "Is he asking for Change, or is he asking for CHANGE? Follow a man as he affects multiple people's lives with just one dollar, proving it doesn't take much to be the change in someone's life."

This film was nominated and won two 2012 Regional Emmy Awards. Roger Ebert raved about it, saying, "It touched me."

I encourage you to look up this short yet inspiring film, and I hope it touches your Heart as it did mine. Time passes, and the circle of life continues on, yet the seeds of kindness and peace you have planted (remember planting them on your movie set?) begin blooming in each of the gardens of those Hearts you have blessed.

There are people who are eternally grateful, who don't know how to express how they feel. Let that be okay. Give of yourself when and where it feels right, trusting your Heart to guide you. Planting, watering, and cultivating seeds of goodness will come back to you multiplied in wondrous ways. And, your movie set will grow much more beautiful because of it.

THE CRITICS

Their names are criticism, judgment, gossip, blame, worry, anger and fear. They are just a few of the critics! This family of negativity turns our vibratory energy into molasses — quicksand to our good, making it extremely difficult to step out of, and just as dangerous.

Choosing to engage in activities of love, peace, harmony, joy and kindness raises vibratory actions, speeding up the magnetization of our good. As you watch inspirational movies or read the many self-help books available, you may become determined to improve the quality of your life. This determination can be short circuited if you keep rewinding and replaying your old movie scenes. The film is probably old, scratched, faded out and ready for the editing floor. Why keep reliving the drama you hope to transform? Habit? Comfort?

Ingrained habits are a challenge to break and have tricky ways of creeping back in, which slows your progress, so constant vigilance is necessary. Changing a habit can be one of the most challenging things you will ever do, so stay determined! If you are serious about change, drop the excuses, and ask yourself why you want to eliminate a particular habit.

Going through the exercise of the W's — what, when, why, where and who — can bring clarity to the habit in question. Ask yourself:

What do I gain from ______________________________?
When did ___________________________ become a habit?
Why do I choose ________________________________?
Where do I think ____________________ will get me in life?
Who are my role models? __________? Are they successful?
Is __________________ really something I want in my life?

Sometimes the answer lies in the question. When you take the time to filter an occurrence or a piece of news through the W's, the right response usually becomes obvious.

It is beneficial to find a positive replacement for any habits you desire to break free of. Affirm daily, "Everything I need is here for me now in this moment. My purpose reveals itself to me in perfect timing. I am the master of my life, and it unfolds exactly as I direct it. I trust in my Higher Power, which is inside me. As I connect with my Source, I become a magnet for ______________."

Write an affirmation supporting every area of your life where you are not free.

When we continue participating with "the critics," lasting peace and joy will be elusive. Understand more, so you fear less. Once you begin shining your joy Light bright, the energy vampires cannot stand to be in your presence! Become a blessing counter, a Light capturer. Take charge, making sure life is not happening to you but through you.

If you think your life is difficult, remember challenges strengthen the Light inside you. Compare your problems to others, and you may view your life from a different perspective. These "tests" of our courage are a call to action. What action you take, well, that's up to you, but staying heart-centered will help you connect to the best solutions. You can set yourself free.

Changing the dialogue in your movie can change your life, so change the conversation, evict the critics along with all their baggage, and embrace the all-knowing perfection of you. The challenge in making lasting change is that you are required to step out of your comfort zone. Have faith in yourself, and if you need help, ask for it.

Last, but not least, it is important to reward yourself for all your accomplishments. Go on, you know you want to! Not only is it fun, it helps prevent relapsing into old habits. If you reward yourself with something that makes you feel good every time you think of it, you will be more inclined to accomplish even more, for ever greater rewards.

THE ONGOING PURSUIT OF PEACE

People say they want to live peacefully in cooperation with each other, but they want the other side to make the first move. Has history taught us nothing? The endless maze of shadows and self-destruction will only end when we wake up and begin walking hand in hand in peaceful cooperation with each other and in our communities. Peace in every area of our life and in the world needs to be a number one priority for all of us before change can occur; only then will we witness a conscious shift worldwide.

Civilizations have been destroyed, because peace could not be sustained. After all we have seen throughout history, why are we no closer to living and loving in peace than we were hundreds and thousands of years ago? One of the main reasons is EGO (Editing God aka Your Good Out.) If everyone connected to the Divine Love and Light in their Hearts in an instant, taking a stand side by side for Oneness, Unity, Grace and Peace, our world would transform instantaneously. What will movies of the future feature about our civilization on Earth?

Many movies, a few mentioned in this book, have been made with this exact theme in Mind. There are peacemakers who have walked this Earth throughout the ages who are held in great esteem, because of their commitment to peace. Thank you to these way-showers, many who have lived challenging lives, yet never gave up the hope of peace prevailing in our world. Their existence has blessed countless lives, bringing Light and illumination to us all.

One of many women who have inspired me is the late Maya Angelou. As an internationally renowned bestselling author, poet, actress and political activist, she has held more than 50 honorary university degrees, truly walked her talk as a bright shining example of courage, and will be remembered throughout the world as a spokesperson for human rights, freedom, justice and peace. In my eyes, Maya Angelou was a courageous, peace-commanding presence — a true, living example loved the world over.

Peace gifts us with the power of transformation, when we have the courage to choose it. Just as in a beautiful garden, those who choose harmlessness add a lovely essence, a sense of peaceful perfection to the world. Anyone whose life purpose is to improve the human condition through compassion, love, knowledge, peace and creativity is a great blessing to all life.

The desired changes we make on the inside will affect significant changes on the outside. Imagine the sheer magnitude of change descending over the world if we all chose to co-exist in peace together. Think about this...it's a game changer! Take a deep look inside to see where you're not choosing peace in your life. As I spoke of earlier, do you react or respond to life's little triggers?

It's easy to see the damage created when people react using the family of fear to handle challenging situations. Wars are a perfect example. They may seem to solve the issues at hand, but in the long run everyone involved is harmed, leaving people and countries separated, broken, disappointed and angry.

We are energy. How we direct our energy affects everyone, everywhere. Creating conflict takes us from peace backward across the bridge to pain, discord, and anger. Over time, the fallout can reappear, manifesting on a larger scale, because it has become even more destructive. When conflict shows up from an old unresolved pain, simply because someone did not listen or reacted unkindly, peace is diluted.

Unless we hold onto uninterrupted peace, individually and collectively, our world as we know it could end up as another movie in the future about a civilization that did not choose peace over discord. The title, *The Earth That Could Have Been; Destroyed by Sheeple People*. In this movie, they put sheep heads on our bodies to illustrate how willingly we followed those who were out to herd us like cattle. Keeping the masses (that would be us) distracted from their true identity of Divine Love, Light, Wisdom and Power, then finally to eliminate as many of us as possible from the movie.

I know, it's creepy, but is it totally out of the realm of possibility? Now imagine this scenario: we all take our power back, standing guard at the gate of our consciousness, constantly vigilant until there are only thoughts of Love, Light, Abundance and Peace. Well, you do the math. No Sheeple in that movie, and the best part, we see an entirely different ending!

If your creative activity was to direct and shoot a film that would make a difference in your life and in your world, what would your movie be about?

ARE YOU LETTING THE OUTER WORLD PULL ON YOU?

It's easy to remain peaceful in a quiet, prayerful, meditative state or while living undisturbed from the inside out. When the outer world pulls on us, and it does, this gives us an opportunity to test our inner strength. Remember — peace is power.

The platform beneath our feet is the perfect classroom to practice honing our peace skills. Putting your best effort into the study of being a good human will not only make a good life for you, but it will also raise your energy levels, frequency patterns, and support the success of the moving picture of your life. Sharing the steps you take to live an excellent life can benefit many people who are looking for answers to the everyday challenges in life.

Choosing to live in peace with ourselves and our precious Mother Earth creates momentum, which in turn carries us into an expanded state of being, connecting us with the Source of our daily good. Our own individualized presence of peace embodies all the qualities of Love and Light, Wisdom and Power, carrying within it the infinite intelligence to create from its own realm of perfection.

> *"Peace. It does not mean to be in a place where there is no noise, trouble, or hard work. It means to be in the midst of those things and still be calm in your heart."*
>
> — Author Unknown

PEACE TIPS

★ Connect with your Heart, listening to the messages you receive.

★ Use your intuition. Rational thinking is essential, but developing your intuitive Mind can aid you in the most effective ways.

★ Connect with a space of stillness and solitude each day for prayer, meditation, quieting the Mind, a visit with nature. Sacred space is a private and personal choice.

★ Engage in something that deeply shifts you into a place of love, peace, and joy. Absorb and carry this feeling with you as you move about your day.

★ Do something of value for others to bring them peace and joy.

★ Disconnect from nonessential distractions. Re-examine the W's — What, When, Why, Where, Who.

★ Love yourself. Look yourself in the mirror and say: "I love you; I choose peace in every moment of this day." Choose a statement that affects you. Creative consistency builds your self-awareness and self-esteem.

★ Be a magnet for peace. Walk your talk. Be a living example.

★ Follow your passion with a peaceful Heart.

★ Choose to live in peace with yourself and our precious Mother Earth. This creates momentum, which in turn carries you into an expanded state of being, connecting you with the Source of your daily good.

MOVIE SCENARIOS — YOURS, MINE, AND OURS

Just for fun, let's look at two different movie scenarios. In the first film, you connect to the all knowing Perfected Presence living inside you (inner world influence) where you live a peaceful, happy life of achievement and joy. The film title is *The Peaceful Life*. In the second film, you go through life on your own, living from the outside in (outer world influences) with hit or miss performances. The title of this film is *The Conflicted Life.*

You and I have the choice to play the lead in either scenario for as long as we want, tasting contrast and pushing the limits. One day the playwright in us says, "This character has had enough exposure to conflict and is ready to live in peace." As we turn our attention to the Perfected Presence inside, which has been patiently waiting for our attention to be turned its way, loving to be our partner in life, our movie begins to unfold beautifully.

As you know, when an audience watches a movie, each person comes away with varied perspectives and can be deeply affected by what they see and feel. We have the extraordinary freedom to give the viewers any type of experience we choose. They can watch us moving from a conflicted life to one of peace, much like a butterfly emerging from the cocoon, transformed into beauty, with wings to fly. The view of our life cycle going through a complete metamorphosis gives courage, hope, and inspiration to those looking for transformation in their lives.

Butterflies are a symbol of fragility and ephemeral beauty. There is strength about them, which we see as courageous, because of their incredible transformation. Not one of us will escape some form of transformation in our lives. We can choose to emerge from the cocoon defeated or victorious.

Contrast is an excellent teacher. Through the experience of contrast, we learn what we do and do not want. Are you taking control as the director of your life? Have you found your purpose? Are you experiencing your passion? How do you want the movie of your life to play out? Our choices have a cause and effect upon the bigger picture of all life. Do you complain, unappreciative throughout the day, finding fault in people, situations and things? If you find yourself feeling grateful for the little things in life, appreciating each moment, as well as all the miracles appearing for you, think about shelving *The Conflicted Life* indefinitely, or put it in the shredder and be done with it. You are now the happy star performer in *The Peaceful Life.*

What a difference these two outlooks make in the production and outcome of the movie you live and star in. All filmmakers know you have to edit, cut, edit, all the while staying in creative mode (pull out your bag of cinematic techniques) in order for the final version of the movie to be a worthwhile endeavor.

Which areas of your life are in need of editing? Is your life harmonious, or are there varying degrees of discord? If you want to star in *The Peaceful Life*, it will take dedication and determination. Your audience will know you went to the editing table cutting out the scenes not serving your best interest or those of the cast of characters in your film. Some will prefer to see *The Conflicted Life* and may have no interest in seeing your movie, just yet. I have a hunch even the popcorn tastes better when viewing *The Peaceful Life*! My favorite is truffle popcorn with grated Parmesan cheese and a sprinkle of chives...addicting.

BE THE EXCEPTION TO THE RULE

As you experience the many aspects of yourself you came here to explore, healing begins. Each day is a new opportunity for self-exploration. Being true to yourself by living an authentic life allows you to own your personal power. Not being a follower makes you an exception to the rule. Copying other people to fit in can steal your personal identity and powerful life force. Trust me; I learned this one the hard way. I wanted approval, for people to "like" me, avoided conflict, and was a pleaser growing up. I was the good kid. I tried to copy others I felt I wanted to be like, because they "seemed" to be more than me. I finally realized I am enough, just as I am at each stage of my growth. We all go through some aspect of trying to fit in, but if you are paying attention, at some point you come to the conclusion we are all exceptional in our own way.

Wisdom is gained, and many lessons are learned from trying to fit in, all part of learning who we are and who we are not. Part of our culture is being taught to conform to the norm. Trying to fit a square peg into a round hole, to fit into another person's kind of lifestyle, can be painful. As people live from the outside in, trying to be like the majority, their authentic inner voice loses the momentum they are meant to connect with and share.

Growing up, we find ourselves wanting to emulate people who exhibit the great qualities we admire. Find those qualities in yourself; add them to your movie-making toolkit, and make them uniquely and authentically your own. Be an exception to the rule, and you will find each day is more peace-full + joy-full = happy! Start by realizing you are wonder-full just as you are. You are enough, I am enough; we all are! We are safe in our authenticity. Hold true to your integrity, ideals, and dreams. Keep on the lookout out for more unique independent films coming your way! They are my favorite movie category.

If you want to change your movie, you have to change your life. In the movie *Billy Elliot*, we see a boy who overcomes prejudices and personal fears, as well as physical and mental pain. This movie is an example of being the exception to the rule, showing how to live authentically despite the odds stacked against you. Billie had a great mentor in Mrs. Wilkinson, who helps keep him strong and focused, even though she has to overcome her own doubts and fears to help him succeed.

This is what great movies are made of, just like "reel" life. When we put our life on hold for another person, place or thing, our lives can become stagnant. Connecting daily to our individualized I AM Source of perfection brings balanced Peace, Love, and Light into all our outer expressions. Growing and nurturing peace within ourselves, those around us, and the world we live in is the best way to build long-lasting relationships, bringing more peace into everything, everywhere.

DEBRA'S STORYBOARD ON PEACE

There are unseen spiritual forces in the Universe that go to work for me when I connect to the powerful "I" that I AM through the energy of thought and feeling in meditation and prayer. By directing this presence with all my Heart and Soul in a loving, peaceful way each morning, I am taking action by pre-paving my day. My job is to hold my peace and allow the powerful forces I have directed to handle the details.

Getting out of my own way (not always easy) and allowing what I have set into motion to process and manifest is the best course of action. This way, my day unfolds perfectly. Are there challenging days? Of course, but for the most part, they are smooth and joyfull. It comes back to me reminding myself to step off the hose so to speak, allowing the unimpeded flow of Love and Light to water the seeds of thought and feeling I have planted.

My goal is to remain peaceful and grateful for all that is here and all that is yet to appear in my life. Old habits are hard to break, but doing so is well worth the effort, and no one said this journey was going to be without its challenges or that we would not require courage to get through some of them. Through challenges, I have experienced many contrasts that have provided growth and expansion for my multi-body system. How I handle challenges determines the outer experiences showing up in the movie of my life.

In a redwood forest with Mother Nature and her kingdoms is, for me, one of the most sacred, peaceful places and spaces. What's yours?

YOUR PERSONAL STORYBOARD ON PEACE

1. What does Peace mean to you?

____

____

____

____

____

2 What does "harmless to self and others for the highest and greatest good" mean to you?

____

____

____

____

____

3. By aligning Mind with Spirit, I recognize I have gained Peace by:

4. Explain the phrase, "What you resist persists."

5. For me, practicing being a Peaceful Warrior means:

6. Instead of engaging in gossip, criticism, judgment and blame, I choose to:

____

____

____

____

____

7. The positive frequencies Peace brings into my life are:

____

____

____

____

____

#6 — TREATMENT FOR SCRIPT ON PEACE

Victor knew his dad, Tony, had been a member of the Southside Torpedoes when he was younger; but he had never talked about it. Tony left the gang when Victor's mom told him she was going to have a baby. Tony had enough respect within the gang and was allowed to get out. They had then moved to an apartment on the north side of the city, and Tony took a job as a night custodian in a local school for gifted children. When Victor was four, his mother taught him to read. When he was five, his dad started taking him to work. Victor would sit in the library reading books while his dad worked.

"Think of the library as a gold mine," Tony often told him. "Knowledge is the key to acquiring wealth, freedom, and a good life."

The school tested Victor and found he had a high IQ; they admitted him on scholarship and Victor excelled. As he entered his junior year, he was already being recruited by major universities. His mother was so proud of him.

Then tragedy rocked Victor's world. A former Torpedo named Chato had gotten out of prison for a jewelry store robbery gone bad 18 years earlier. Now considered a Veterano, (a respected elder of his former gang) Tony had been on the lookout and warned the other gang members when he heard the police sirens approaching. Chato blamed Tony as the reason he got caught, but the truth was Chato had lingered to grab more jewelry and couldn't run as fast. The police chased him down, and he went to prison. Chato had vowed revenge.

Late one night, as Victor and his father were coming out of the school, a car full of Southside Torpedoes rolled up, and Chato put a gun out of the car window. Tony only had enough time to push his son down to the ground, shielding Victor as the bullets tore into his own body. As Tony lay dying, his last words to his son were,

"Don't blame Chato. We all pay for our sins. Take care of your mother."

Victor is devastated. He feels anguish begin to turn to anger and lets it boil over into vengeance. When the police arrive, he lies and tells them he didn't see anything and doesn't know who did this. Victor begins plotting his revenge against Chato and the other Torpedoes. His mother pleads with him not to go down the path of revenge. He ignores her.

He learns the Torpedoes biggest rival gang is the Winamac Warriors, who control most of the north side of the city. Victor drops out of school and joins the Warriors. He puts his intellect to use doubling their profits in two short years and laundering the money through several front businesses. He is rewarded with drink, drugs, girls, anything he desires; but he only wants one thing.

On a dark November night, Victor is driven to a warehouse along the river. Inside, the Warriors have Chato tied to a chair. One of them hands Victor a gun. Victor puts the gun in Chato's mouth and looks him in the eyes, laughing at the man's fear; but, before he can pull the trigger, the police raid the warehouse. Victor is arrested and convicted under the RICO statutes. He is sentenced to 30 years in Joliet Prison and, five days after arriving, he is stabbed to death in the laundry. His mother is heartbroken.

FADE TO BLACK

#6 — REWRITE OF TREATMENT FOR SCRIPT ON PEACE

Victor knew his dad, Tony, had been a member of the Southside Torpedoes when he was younger; but he had never talked about it. Tony left the gang when Victor's mom told him she was going to have a baby. Tony had enough respect within the gang and was allowed to get out. They had then moved to an apartment on the north side of the city, and Tony took a job as a night custodian in a local school for gifted children. When Victor was four, his mother taught him to read. When he was five, his dad started taking him to work. Victor would sit in the library reading books while his dad worked.

"Think of the library as a gold mine," Tony often told him. "Knowledge is the key to acquiring wealth, freedom, and a good life."

The school tested Victor and found he had a high IQ; they admitted him on scholarship and Victor excelled. As he entered his junior year, he was already being recruited by major universities. His mother was so proud of him.

Then tragedy rocked Victor's world. A former Torpedo named Chato had gotten out of prison for a jewelry store robbery gone bad 18 years earlier. Now considered a Veterano, (a respected elder of his former gang) Tony had been on the lookout and warned the other gang members when he heard the police sirens approaching. Chato blamed Tony as the reason he got caught, but the truth was Chato had lingered to grab more jewelry and couldn't run as fast. The police chased him down, and he went to prison. Chato had vowed revenge.

Late one night, as Victor and his father were coming out of the school, a car full of Southside Torpedoes rolled up, and Chato put a gun out of the car window. Tony only had enough time to push his son down to the ground, shielding Victor as the bullets tore into his own body. As Tony lay dying, his last words to his son were,

"Don't blame Chato. We all pay for our sins. Take care of your mother."

Victor is devastated. He feels anguish begin to turn to anger but remembers his mother telling him anger is a bad road going downhill. When the police arrive, he tells the detective what he saw and what his father had said. The carload of Torpedoes are pulled over and arrested before they can get back to their home turf. Chato is convicted of murder. The other gang members received lighter sentences as accessories to the crime. The gang never retaliated because they knew Chato was a loose cannon who had the cops knocking at their door too much, and they all knew it was his fault for getting caught. Tony had done his job.

Victor goes to college and studies urban social problems. He graduates and returns to his neighborhood where he starts a program teaching at-risk kids to read, write, and basic life skills. His program also teaches them about their human worth, their potential, and the power of peace. The program succeeds and goes nationwide in just a few years. Crime rates noticeably drop in cities across the country, especially the murder rate for teens. Victor is a featured guest at the State of the Union address where the President gives him credit for the change.

His mother is so proud of him.

FADE TO WHITE

REEL WRAP: THE CONCEPT OF PEACE

- ★ Peace is strength in action. Peace is power.
- ★ Do you find yourself responding or reacting to life? You may edit or rewrite your personal script whenever needed.
- ★ When you continue participating with "the critics," lasting peace and joy will be elusive.
- ★ Give of yourself when and where it feels right, trusting your Heart to guide you. Planting, watering, and cultivating seeds of goodness will come back to you multiplied in wondrous ways.
- ★ Look deep inside to see where you're not choosing peace in your life.
- ★ Live uniquely and authentically. Be an exception to the rule, and you will find each day is more peace-full + joy-full = happy! Start by realizing you are wonder-full just as you are. You are enough, I am enough, and we all are!
- ★ Peace gifts you the power of transformation.

Concept #7: RHYTHM

Are You Ready to Put Your Movie Together?

"The potential hidden within you is staggering. Shed the old layers, and devote yourself to something of value that sings to the passion in your Soul. Now you become the master of your destiny."

— Debra Oakland

Sustaining anything requires rhythm. The 7 Concepts in this book are put together in such a way that, when they are combined and used consistently, they will enhance the quality of your life. Think of life as a sacred, rhythmic dance choreographed by you to create your personal symphony. One of the most important components in any great movie is the rhythm of the music, which dramatically enhances the story line. This is where an ordinary movie becomes extraordinary!

Learning the use and application of Universal Laws and Principles in a rhythmic manner helps bring our desires into form and, like all things that grow, it is good to regularly feed the desire we wish to birth. Consistency is essential to the success of our desire manifesting and will determine the length of its duration in our life.

Choose one desire you wish to bring into your outer reality, and then apply these concepts for a reality shift.

Everything in life has a rhythm establishing cycles, patterns, and different stages of development. Our heartbeat and breathing are perfect examples. Mother Nature flows in rhythmic relationship, season to season. There are great cosmic rhythms in our ever-expanding Universe. Rhythmic waves bind together, creating matter.

SACRED SPACE

> *"The same stream of life that runs through my veins night and day runs through the world and dances in rhythmic measures."*
>
> — Rabindranath Tagore

Our lives expand exponentially when we connect daily in a rhythmic way to the Source of our good. Patterns are created which form our world from the inside out. Sacred space is where we go to form and express those secret, sacred parts of us we experience as life.

Those who enter into sacred space regularly are familiar with deep, rhythmic breathing techniques that soothe the Body, Mind, and Spirit, clearing discord and calming emotions that may be stirred up. Notice when someone is angry or fearful, they forget to breathe, causing tension throughout the body. In contrast, breathing in and out with relaxed intention, while in a state of peace, is healing.

One of the most important benefits of cleansing, healing and breathing is the all-powerful connection to our inner Source of Love, Wisdom, and Power. Many forms of breathing techniques are used for spiritual practices, yoga, childbirth, singing, sports, stress, etc. Rhythmic breath is our friend, there to assist us in many ways.

Adding focus and intention to our breathing has even more advantages. If you are interested in breathing techniques, Conscious Breathing Coach Gay Hendricks has written wonderful books on the power of breathing and its importance in our lives. He teaches his techniques around the world and is considered an expert trainer. The Internet is a great Source of information on this subject.

OUR RHYTHMS ARE CREATED FROM CHILDHOOD

Children enter this world feeling the power of possibilities and that dreams can come true. A small child does not understand the concept of limitation. At the earliest stage of development, they are taught the idea of limits.

Don't climb up there; you will fall.

Don't touch that; you will burn yourself.

We don't do that, because it ____________________.

Don't do that; I am afraid you will ________________.

Although these are phrases uttered by loving and well-meaning parents who want to protect their child from harm, they can be the introduction to limitation and fear.

Awareness of how and what we teach children shapes them for life. Take, for instance, a father who has never tried anything that pushes limits. Day after day, he comes home from work at about the same time, has a drink, watches the news, eats dinner, watches the same shows on television, and has no clue about the listless, boring, and meaningless example he is setting for his children. The tipping point comes when resentment, frustration, and fear accumulate year after year until the child acts out in protest and rejection of their father's way of life. The undoing is almost as painful as the lifetime of habits that were put into place. Although it is a given that we need to protect children from harm's way, bringing them up with confidence, curiosity, and a passion for life rarely results in childhood traumas and splintered families.

If we start out with a framework of "don't" and "shouldn't" as children (remember, it's not nice to "should" on people!), we grow and develop habits or rhythms that can deter or stifle our life path. Most infants' needs and wants are few and simple. As a child develops, being fed the concepts of "reality" in regular doses often results in the Heart's greatest dreams and desires being set aside. At this point, they begin to believe in the limitations taught to them by people who were fed those same limitations as they developed in a seemingly limited world.

Turning our intention and attention away from creating rhythmically to what we were told might not be possible causes us to feel vital parts of our dreams slipping away. The business of life and its illusion of limitation carry many adults in its grasp, creating a rhythm quite different from the one they dreamed of living. In most cases, the original unlimited dreams of childhood were long forgotten or put on a shelf to attend to later.

There are many fortunate people who never gave up their dreams and do feel anything is possible for them. They were strengthened in some way, some through encouragement, some through pure tenacity and determination. What a blessing! This is not so for the majority of the population but is beginning to shift as people wake up to their passion and limitless potential.

Later in life, you see people taking action to salvage parts of the original rhythmic imagination of childhood that had brought them such incredible feelings of joy and anticipation all those years ago. With wisdom gained after years of abandoning the dreams of childhood, people become thrilled at the opportunity to take their dreams off the shelf. The creative process of feeling unlimited comes back as we shift the focus from any fear and doubt that suppressed the dreams to the immense thrill of dreaming in an unlimited way once again, that's what great movies are made of!

We can create new neuro networks and pathways in the brain simply by changing our Mind, which changes the way the neuro pathways operate. So, at any point in our lives, we can take our dream off the shelf and give it new life, or find another one which brings us joy. It is our nature to feel good and a responsible choice.

Letting go of fear-based programming, reaching for our dreams and desires in a conscious way, returns us to our authentic roots, the true nature of who and what we are. When we make a concentrated effort to connect to our Hearts and trust we know what is right for us, just as we did as a child, we will find creativity ready to spill out of us and into our dreams manifest. This "you" will not function in the structure of the outside world as it once did. Releasing fear and doubt gifts you with a new outlook on life, showing the endless possibilities available. Rhythmically creating with purpose while on purpose, makes it is easier to reconnect with your dreams and to express in your own unique way.

RHYTHM, REPETITION & LITTLE BROTHERS!

There is rhythm flowing in and out of our lives. For example, I grew up reading. I loved the look, feel, and smell of books and the magical words they held. Paper, pencils, pens and anything to do with writing made my senses come alive. Reading was sacred to me. I began my search for truth and unity at an early age, as I did not understand the injustice out in the world. Much of what I was told or saw "out there" did not make sense. My solar plexus would tense up when I heard something that felt out of line with integrity or caused me to doubt and question.

I learned to trust those feelings, which have served me very well. I searched for my passion out in the world, and later in life I found it right where I had placed it, inside me. Had I paid attention much earlier to the clues that I had excellent typing skills all through school, could pass a class writing poetry, loved bookstores, writing personal journals, reading and collecting books, I might have written more consistently and shared my writing sooner. Here is a little history of my youth.

My brother Ted was three years my junior. When we were young, he would follow me around endlessly and, like older children often do, I told him to go away and leave me alone. This is a normal childhood situation for anyone with siblings. I was the oldest, and then my brothers and sisters, Ted, Tim, Trish and Kara, followed. Our parents would deal with our squabbles the best way they could, but kids will be kids! The more I would try to get rid of Ted, the more he would tell me I was stupid.

In his Mind, this must have been his only recourse. I understand that now but did not at the time. Ted would tell me I was stupid or I could not do a particular thing, because I was a girl, and to him all girls had cooties. He would put a big black X on himself and his toys as protection against girl cooties. All silly and harmless, yet I absorbed the "You are stupid" comments on a deep level.

At a young age, I didn't understand kids at school laugh at everything and tease each other relentlessly. I would raise my hand in answer to a question from the teacher, and when other children laughed, I thought it was because I was stupid. I quit asking or answering too many questions in class throughout elementary school, in case I answered wrong, making me look and feel stupid. Then I quit listening in class. I shut down part of my vital creative rhythmic flow by not taking the risk to be heard.

I became social in junior high and high school and was successful in that area. School was a place to have fun. My grades were poor, not because I was stupid, but because I did not apply myself. I'm good at what I apply myself to.

As an avid reader all my life, I also enjoyed writing. I'm sure you know where this is headed! I believed smart, educated people could be writers and authors, and since I did not feel smart, it made sense to give up writing. After high school, I fell into a rhythm of life I thought served me best, and it did at the time. Years later as an adult and many life changes later, I began looking at my other passions, taking photography and art classes, thinking about design school, and becoming involved in the fashion business.

Although I enjoyed my time while all of this was going on, I was not fulfilled at my deepest Soul level of expression. After losing five immediate family members in a short period of time, something powerful awakened in me. I decided it was time to write and share what I had learned throughout those years. Voila! Joyful fulfillment!

Every day I say to myself: "I am unlimited. I am a successful author with a powerful voice." I had put my dream aside, while I consistently wore "I can't see you" glasses! Here I am, full circle back to my passion, which has been showing up rhythmically throughout my life. I believed in a self-imposed limitation of thought. Would I change the life I have lived? No; not a moment of it. Every experience and challenge (of which there were many!) led me back to my passion and was instrumental to my growth, assisting me in becoming the person I am today. Gratitude? You bet!

It's never too late to reinvent yourself. Writing has connected me to people all over the world, changing my life in ways I can't begin to explain. I love what I do. It is my passion. I don't compare myself to other writers, because we all have our own unique voice, and the gift in each voice is to express authentically. One of the pleasures of reading and writing are the endless choices and voices! I met my contributing author, Steve Tallamy, online through writing. Steve writes about Mother Nature. Guess what he spent his childhood doing? Loving nature and exploring her kingdoms. Now he writes with passion about his passion.

WHOSE RHYTHM ARE YOU LIVING TO?

Growing up, I often found myself trying to live to the rhythm of other people. The advertisements in magazines, television, movies and all manner of media have most people thinking they need to be like, or live like, the people in the ads, movies, or television shows — or at least a close facsimile. I discovered most of those outer world rhythms to be contrived and controlling. Keep people from thinking for themselves and they are easy to control. There are powerful people out there who have done a great disservice to all.

Because humans have free will, we learn from the great teachings of "contrast." The outer world is enticing, yet people are dancing to their own rhythm in increasing numbers. I have joined the dance and find it enchanting, exciting, and educational. By loving ourselves and our humanity, we carry a greater sense of freedom, because we are rhythmically living and loving ourselves from the inside out.

The outer world loses its grip on us when we connect with and apply Universal Laws and Principles as a daily rhythmic practice.

It takes our attention and intention to disengage from the outer world and its controlling forces, but it is worth the time and effort, for the benefits are indescribable as you connect to the inner world of your personal power and authenticity.

It is our birthright to live in abundance, joy, and peace. Material things in the world are wonderful and can bring us great satisfaction. It is the "attachment" to these things through EGO that can place people in some unsavory, self-inflicted situations. By thinking the "only" access to our good is through another person, place, or thing, we lose ourselves in a fearful, tail-chasing race. On the other hand, when directing our life from the inside, where the "true" access to all our good exists, life supplies us with what we need right when we need it.

Holding tight to what is "mine, not yours" does not serve us for long or bring lasting joy into our lives. Giving, sharing, and being of value and service do bring lasting joy. Since we are all One, when giving to another, we give to ourselves. A strong connection with our Higher Inner Power gives us greater access to direct this powerful force of Love we have come here to express in the outer world for all our needs and desires. Trust in the natural abundance of the Universe, and allow gratitude to blissfully shower you with blessings.

You and I have been given the choice to connect with and learn to master the Power we have been gifted. This Power is alive, expressing itself uniquely through each of us. Permanent satisfaction in all that can be amassed in the outer world is elusive. There is a permanent sense of accomplishment and satisfaction in manifesting one's life purpose through the rhythmic and accomplished use of Universal Laws and Principles.

Careful and deliberate co-creation through cooperation can be rhythmically repeated with continued success. It is important to guide each other back to our individualized Source of Power. The answers we look for the world over are right here, at home in our Heart, Soul, and Spirit, where they have always been.

DISCARD THOSE OLD WORN-OUT RHYTHMS

Breaking free of old worn-out habits is like stepping out of quicksand onto a solid foundation. A new perspective is refreshing, giving personal transformation a more positive outlook. Take the time to create space for your desired shifts to take hold. In the wise words of Mark Twain, "Loyalty to a petrified opinion never yet broke a chain or freed a human soul."

When an old habit comes up and attempts to take control, take a look at it, recognize it, process it and let it go. By rhythmically acknowledging and releasing, we are mastering a new area of our life, as well as raising our vibrational frequency. A true breath of fresh air, full of grace and peace, brings about our Mind unfolding in a unique, personal, and private realignment.

Since everything is energy, using our energy rhythmically in the new frequencies will assist us greatly in times to come. Any skill takes practice, and working with energy is no different. Reversing patterns can be easier in some areas than others. As we become more skilled, we build momentum for great change and manifestation. Will there be moments of frustration and challenge? You bet! As positive momentum builds and new skills are put to use, frustration fades into thin air, making time and space for joyful creating of the life you plan to live.

We are limitless souls on a human journey who are capable of changing our lives in any way we desire. Absolute power is ours over our own destiny. Each one will open the door to personal transformation when they are ready. No one is farther ahead or behind, for this is a personal journey unique to each of us and cannot be forced, or compared to the path of another. No one will be left behind in the return to collective Oneness.

Life experiences bring us to a time and place when we just "know." Knowingness alights something in us that burns a freedom flame of passion for self-discovery in the return to Divine Love and Light. We have many identities in the outer world but only one that matters — Love.

It is in our best interest, and the intention of this book, to encourage people to live from the inside out, versus the outside in, so when we work on self-exploration, the "aha" moments that come are more powerful, meaningful, and longer lasting. This is your movie, so treat it with respect and patience, because it belongs exclusively to you and you alone.

By reaching outside your comfort zone, you will get used to varying degrees of being "uncomfortable." Be aware through the growing and birthing pains there is much to be grateful for. This is all part of the bigger journey we all traverse together as we strive toward an understanding of ourselves and our Universe.

We truly are magnificent spirits, creator beings housed in these physical garments.

DEBRA'S STORYBOARD ON RHYTHM

Sitting relaxed and breathing rhythmically until I feel connected, I talk to my Perfected Higher Self through thought and feeling. Quietly or out loud, I say: "Everything is flowing in, through, and around me as my life is abundant, joyful, healthy, peaceful, harmonious, and full of unity and grace. I express appreciation for this magnificent, powerful force of Love. My highest goal is to pre-pave my life movie through thought, feeling, and action, then to remain harmonious and peaceful, trusting in my Higher Power to handle the details, seen and unseen. I live in gratitude for all that is here and all that is yet to come."

YOUR PERSONAL STORYBOARD ON RHYTHM

1. Upon awakening in the morning, I am consciously aware of the Rhythm in:

____

____

____

____

____

2. In my personal daily spiritual ritual, I acknowledge Rhythm by:

____

____

____

____

____

3. By aligning Mind with Spirit, I recognize I am free to:

____

____

____

____

____

4. As I start my daily walk, I will focus my attention on Rhythmic living regarding:

____

____

____

____

____

5. The musical styles or songs best representing the Rhythm of my day are:

6. In Light and Love, I recognize and acknowledge this new principle operating in my life in these areas:

7. I choose to engage in positive Rhythmic frequencies by:

#7 — TREATMENT FOR SCRIPT ON RHYTHM

FADE IN:

Dancing! Oh, how I love to dance. Movement fills me, my body sings in silence, washing away all else. I am born to dance, to tell a story. Have you ever wanted to do something with such passion that the rest of your life slips away in comparison? The Heart and Soul of a dancer is aligned with the rhythm of music, transferring the entire Universe of that individual to another world as they become lost in dance for a time, yet fully present in the moment, interpreting the movement.

I love ballet. My goal is to become the premier ballerina of the New York City Ballet. That has driven me since I started dancing as a child. I have attended every class, danced in every recital and ballet, dedicated myself to being the best dancer around, and I put in the grueling years of training to be in the position to audition for and be accepted into the School of American Ballet.

What a shock when I arrive. I was the premier dancer in my hometown. So were all of the other girls in my class. I must work even harder if I am going to have a chance of even getting in corps de ballet. So many girls are prettier than me, thinner than me, better dancers than me. It is all I can do to keep up my class schedule and work at my night job as a waitress.

I share an apartment with three other dancers, but I don't have the resources they have. Every day is a struggle. I'm not eating well.

I'm pushing myself to the limit, but I feel like I'm not keeping up. The teachers don't correct me. They don't even look at me. I must be a pathetic dancer in their eyes. I'm so tired I can't even feel the music anymore. All I feel is the pain in my leaden legs and my clomping, uncoordinated feet.

Finally the casting is posted for The Nutcracker. I look down the list. There I am in Act I. I'm neighbor No. 6. That's the couple in the back corner in the party scene. What about Act II? Yes, I see my name again. What's this? I'm one of the mice. All of the years of hard work and I am just a stupid mouse?

As I walk home from class, I begin crying. It's just not fair! I hate my life! I'm a failure! What's that Light? A cab!!!!

What happened? Where am I? My entire body feels numb… and cold. All these red and blue flashing lights — I can't seem to move my right leg. I don't think I'm in Des Moines anymore.

FADE TO BLACK

#7 — REWRITE OF TREATMENT FOR SCRIPT ON RHYTHM

FADE IN:

Dancing! Oh, how I love to dance. Movement fills me, my body sings in silence, washing away all else. I am born to dance, to tell a story. Have you ever wanted to do something with such passion the rest of your life slips away in comparison? The Heart and Soul of a dancer is aligned with the rhythm of music, transferring their entire Universe to another world as they become lost in dance for a time, yet fully present in the moment, interpreting the movement.

I love ballet. My goal since I started dancing as a child has been to become the premier ballerina of the New York City Ballet. I have attended every class, danced in every recital and ballet, dedicated myself to being the best dancer around, and I put in many grueling years of training to be in the position to audition for and be accepted into the School of American Ballet.

What a shock when I arrive. I was the premier dancer in my hometown. So were all the other girls in my class. I must work even harder if I am going to have a chance of even getting in corps de ballet. So many girls are prettier than me, thinner than me, better dancers than me. It is all I can do to keep up my class schedule and work at my night job as a waitress.

I share an apartment with three other dancers, but I don't have the resources they have. I decide if I am going to make it, I'm going to have to find a rhythm for my life and stick to it. I make sure I am eating right. I walk everywhere. I make sure I get enough sleep and don't spend too much time partying with my roommates on the weekend. One of them even complimented me on my discipline. I feel like I'm barely keeping up in class, but the teachers are correcting me, which means they notice me. I feel like I am becoming stronger physically and technically as a dancer. I get into the flow of the music, and it seems to take me above the aching joints and tired muscles.

Finally the casting is posted for The Nutcracker. I look down the list. There I am in Act I. I'm neighbor No. 6. That's the couple in the back corner in the party scene. What about Act II? No, but I'm in Scene 3 as one of the snowflakes! And there! I see my name again. I'm in "The Dance of the Flowers." All the years of hard work have paid off! I'm a dancer in the New York City Ballet production of The Nutcracker. Sure, they're small roles, but I feel as if this is just the beginning for me.

As I walk home from class, I begin crying. I'm so happy. I can't wait to call home and tell my mother the news. What's that Light? A cab!!!!

Whew! That was a close one. I better stay focused. I'm definitely not in Des Moines anymore.

FADE TO WHITE

REEL WRAP: THE CONCEPT OF RHYTHM

★ Consistency & Rhythm are essential to the success of your desire manifesting.

★ Use Rhythmic Application of the 7 Concepts.

★ Practice Rhythmic breathing techniques. They soothe the Body, Mind, and Spirit, clearing discord and calming emotions that may be stirred up.

★ If possible take time in the morning and again at night to concentrate on your desired outcome, undisturbed, and then carry it with you throughout the remainder of the day.

★ Whatever you concentrate on, you will bring into your life, so make an effort to feel your best each day.

★ Choose one main desire to focus on that supports all life.

★ Never give up. Be patient and have faith in your desired outcome.

Epilogue
OUT TAKES OF THE 7 REEL CONCEPTS
for Courageous Change

"These 7 Concepts are facets of a spiritual diamond that is Courage."

— Debra Oakland

CONCEPT 1 — CONSCIOUS CHOICE

Choice plus creative action brings our one main desire into fruition. Although we have many desires, it is best to choose and act on the one that fires you up with passion, and one you can concentrate on rhythmically. Start with something that makes sense to you and is not so big your Mind can't accept it or you will not be able to stand in your knowingness it will manifest into form. If you choose a new car, living environment, relationship or perfect health and don't believe it is achievable, there is a good possibility you will fail.

Our multi-body system must be in a state of knowingness that you can and will achieve your desired outcome. Imagine yourself on your movie set, and see this one desire on the screen of your Mind in living color. Step out of fear and doubt, fire "the critics," and make choices in support of all life. Review Concept #1

CONCEPT 2 — WISDOM

Wisdom requires an open Mind. Humans bond strongly with others who uphold their beliefs and concepts. Separation can occur when people disagree. Entire lifetimes are spent defending the concepts of being right. Where is the wisdom in a closed Mind and Heart? Being respectful of other belief systems allows for personal expansion and growth.

The bridge to freedom is within each of us, and we have a right to explore the God of our knowing in any way we choose. Look to people who wisely inspire you without Ego, people who are living examples. They are the shining STARS in their own magnificent movie and encourage you to do the same.

Live authentically. Be less concerned with the opinions of others by welcoming wisdom's warm embrace, which reflects the wonder and creativity in you. Feed your hopes, not your fears. We each have a lifetime of wisdom gained. The question is, how will we share our wisdom with others, and how will we give back with an attitude of gratitude? Review Concept #2

CONCEPT 3 — LOVE

Love is the greatest Power in the Universe. Love carries the highest vibrational frequency and lives inside you. The Law of Love is nutrition for the Body, Mind, and Spirit, the creative force in the Universe that can bring forth the manifestations of your Heart's desires. Use your imagination, dream and create using all your senses, they are there to guide you. See your desire here "NOW," not lost somewhere in the past or out in the future. Remember your Naturally Occurring Wonder belongs to YOU!

Leave old unwanted baggage behind. Release anything keeping you shackled to habits you want to change. Take responsibility for all areas of your life. The blame game is over. Focus like a laser beam on Love. Connect to the power-full magnetic qualities of Love, and put them in your movie. Pay Love forward as you radiate joy out into the world. Love has no borders. Love does not care what color, nationality, race or sex you are. Love just is. Divine Love is unconditional Love — simply said, Love without conditions. Review Concept #3

CONCEPT 4 — PURITY

Purity is a quality that can help set you free from limitation and enhance every area of your life. Your ability to absorb and reflect Light gives you the opportunity to become a mirror displaying your shining brilliance. You are powerful, and by feeling the connection to your strength and power you can defy weakness and powerlessness. Strive to be your best each day.

Everyone has a different standard of purity that resonates with their life path. Set your own standard. What qualities of purity are important to you? The sleeping Soul will wake up when "directed" (remember, this is your movie set, your movie, your life) to activate life toward conscious, uplifting activities.

Purity of Mind comes through patience and perseverance, and sometimes we all need a good purity polish. With this discipline comes the power of momentum as your life moves forward in a much more consistent manner conducive to your happiness. Review Concept #4

CONCEPT 5 — CONCENTRATED ILLUMINATION

Concentrated illumination is concentrated energy infused with Light, that would be you! This puts you in the director's chair of your movie. Your use of this concentrated energetic Light will determine the outcome of your life.

Try some spiritual sunbathing and, while you are soaking up the Light, use your thought to create the life you want to live. Thought is an important element in concentrated illumination, a gateway to your powerful Perfected Presence, the Universal Mind of Love, Wisdom and Power (or the absence of it).

Your creative Power is as unlimited as you are, and simply by setting it into motion, life expands in a joyous way. Find what sparks your core of creativity, and connect with it as you ride the wave all the way to completion. Become the master of your destiny through your own creative Power wanting to express through you. You carry a gift unique only to you. Allow the world to enjoy YOU in all you choose to create.

How is the clarity in your camera lens? Do you need to revise your script, set up auditions, and build a new set design or to silence the negative critics? Are you enjoying the clips you are currently able to view? Life is ever changing, as is your movie, so there is always some editing to be attended to. The life of a movie director is a busy one, so remember to take care of your physical, mental, and spiritual health each day. Review Concept #5

CONCEPT 6 — PEACE

Peace is active and magnetic. Choosing peace taps us directly into our inner Power Station. Peace is our action hero, a concentrated activity bringing harmony into every space it occupies. It takes the power of our attention to hold peace in a world still less than peaceful. Peace is active, and if we wish to have it, we must participate with it. By becoming a living conductor of peace, not only will you be a blessing to the world, you will also be blessed. Peace is power.

Connect with a space of stillness and solitude each day. Sacred space is a private and personal choice. Whether it be prayer, meditation, quieting the mind or a visit with nature, the Universal Intelligence inside you knows how to handle the details as you hold your peace and allow the seen and unseen forces to go to work on your behalf. Review Concept #6

CONCEPT 7 — RHYTHM

> *"When the Universe asks you to dance, say YES!!!"*
>
> Debra Oakland

MY ENCOURAGEMENT TO YOU — HEART TO HEART

I encourage you to dream, to use your imagination daily, envisioning all you desire. Mark Twain said: "You cannot depend on your eyes when your imagination is out of focus."

Remember to see your vision as here and NOW, not lost somewhere in the past or out in the future. See, feel, and experience all of it, using your senses in full living color.

Let Love guide you, impressing vivid images of all you desire to experience with sharp clarity upon your IMAGination movie screen. Choosing to live in the present moment is refreshing. NOW = your Naturally Occurring Wonder! Your life is more exciting, full of endless possibilities and limitless potential. Dragging your old baggage around is like being a vaudeville performer; different stage, but always the same old scenery, the same old costume, same old song and dance.

This simple quote by Louise Smith captures it perfectly:

> *"You can't reach for anything new if your hands are still full of yesterday's junk."*

Why would you choose to keep yourself shackled to all those past lines and worn-out lyrics, when you can choose to shoot your movie on location in living color and Surround Sound? Let your IMAGination live large, love large, and explore all the angles of your life until you get the shot capturing the grandeur and the majesty of who you truly are. Rhythmically live your life breathing in Love, Light, Laughter, Joy, Health and Abundance. Thank you for visiting my personal movie set. I am honored and grateful!

REEL THOUGHTS

It's a Wrap!

> *"Challenges are put in our pathway not to discourage us but to call up the qualities of courage required to find the opportunity in the challenge."*
>
> — Debra Oakland

We are all the same, yet different in our beliefs, paths, and approaches to life. Thank you for taking the time to read this book and for being open to exploring life through the perspective of a movie. These 7 Concepts create a strong foundation and can be used for a lifetime. We all need strong support systems in place for those difficult times we come face to face with. Everyone has challenges, some more painful than others. I survived some very painful years of loss. Using these Universal Laws and Principles pulled me up out of the quicksand and taught me to thrive. If I did it, I believe others can as well. Different tools help us along the way. My hope is this book gives you some valuable tools to include in your movie-making toolbox. I look forward to seeing you at the movies!

OUR TRUE ESSENCE — MY TAKEAWAY FROM WRITING THIS BOOK

This book was one of my greatest teachers. My true essence is the God in me. Divine Presence and I are never separate, yet we operate with different perspectives. The God I AM in me knows and accepts its perfection. I, on the other hand, tend to forget my greatest qualities of perfection. There I go asking, contemplating, meditating, and searching for answers to life's biggest questions, as my Higher Self in its infinite wisdom patiently waits for me to have my "Aha" moments of enlightenment.

No wonder we frustrate ourselves in the quest for spiritual well-being and alignment. Sometimes I have a laugh with myself. It's like "Really, Debra, you are going through this again?" as I pick myself up and move up and out of the old energy I had reattached to for reasons I can only guess, but also understand there is a higher purpose to.

God is in me; God is in you, everywhere present. The best use of my power is to go inside, where I deeply connect to the Source of my personal power. This Source is where I reconnect with my human excellence, which assists me to begin liberating myself from self-imposed limitations. Do I get it right every time? No, I do not, but when I stay vigilant, forward movement occurs.

Part of the process is making powerful choices and decisions while resting in the knowledge all is coming together for my highest good. I also take the action needed on my part. The outcome is a mutual collaboration with my Higher Self. It is my greatest hope, since we are all connected as one, each movement forward for me is one for you in some way. We can make a difference in each other's lives by recognizing our true essence and spreading Light out into the world to each other.

To know myself is to know the God within. I often talk about the creator being in each of us. We are constantly creating by our very thoughts, feelings, and actions. The question is, "What am I creating?" What are you creating? Our time would be well spent mastering a shift in perspective, as well as erasing any limitations keeping us from a strong connection to our individualized Power Source.

Imagine what conscious, creative alignment could bring to those of us willing to make a shift, a transition. Once the process begins, it takes shape organically. The negativity starts to fall away, life gets sweeter every day (you know the song), joy settles in comfortably, life purpose begins to reveal itself, and you start feeling lighter, more confident as creative energy flows in, through, and out from you.

Wow, who would not want this? I would like to think we all do. At this stage, greed gives way to non-attachment based abundance, hope, unity and grace. A whole different intention around abundance, wealth, and opulence fills us. The recognition is, in our connection with each other through love, no one needs to suffer at the hands of another. The Ego is no longer directing the show, saying: "Look at me. I am better than you. I have more than you. I am more than you...so look, look, look at me." A new sheriff shows up with a better way to live and love ourselves and this planet we all share.

Compassion replaces indifference. Love tears down the walls of fear. Serenity and peace become the order of the day. Although our destinations are the same, the paths getting there are wildly varied, as is our reason for being here. It is in our best interest to withhold judgment of anyone's personal preferences in how they reach their destination. Take care to manage your own life to the best of your ability. If we can respect the perfect route for ourselves and our fellow travelers, we are taking the high road, which leads to our highest and greatest good. Human interference has gotten us into some challenging times. May we courageously triumph over our darkest hours and turn them into our most shining moments.

Shift and transform!

A Short Film
NATURE INTERLUDE:
Through the Lens of the Camera

AN INTRODUCTION TO STEVE TALLAMY'S *NATURE INTERLUDE*

This movie short by Steve Tallamy, my contributing author, is a gem. We all share life on Mother Earth together. Steve gives us a powerful overview of each of the 7 Reel Concepts in relation to Mother Earth and nature, a viewing perspective through a different lens you will appreciate. Steve Tallamy has stepped into the role as the author of Nature Interlude – Through the Lens of the Camera. I know you will love his "take" on Mother Nature.

I met Steve many years ago online. Our mutual pursuit of happiness brought us together and has forged a strong alliance and friendship which has grown over the years. Steve lives in the UK.

Steve and I are presenting these 7 Reel Concepts with a different view on the same subject. Contemplating how Mother Nature lives and breathes in her perfect organic way, gives us clues to follow. Nature is our greatest role model and teacher. Steve's perspective, unique expression, and appreciation of Mother Nature complements my message. This book would not be complete without his infinite wisdom, his love of Mother Nature, and the gifts she offers us daily. In each of the 7 Concepts, Steve will be sharing his Nature Interlude as well as his daily personal "Storyboard" of spiritual techniques.

INTRODUCTION BY STEVE TALLAMY

Connecting with Debra was like a stepping stone back into my childhood, a place I had revisited from time to time on my life's journey but hadn't grasped hold of and nurtured for far too many years. We shared secrets and laughed about absolutely nothing, and we still act like school kids whenever we meet today.

In reflection, spending time with Debra was like traveling back to a time when the seeds were sown that made me the person I was, enabling me to do some weeding to become the person I am becoming now.

Born the youngest of four children (by nine years) to loving parents, I never went without, although life was tough for them at the time, and Dad nurtured strict Victorian values. The age difference between me and my siblings didn't seem to be a problem until they became teenagers and I was the snotty-nosed four year old they didn't want to hang around with if they could help it. In retrospect, I cannot blame them for that!

Then an event happened that was to change my life. We bought a cute, black Labrador dog, and he became the best friend a four year old could ever wish for. We lived on a small holding on the outskirts of town on the banks of a quiet, unromantic river. It was a working river, not the sort of river you'd want to swim in, although of course my new buddy and I did. We roamed the banks together, adventurers and pioneers of a new world — Nature's World. I noticed the way he would stop, smell the air, listen and even taste everything around him, and I started to do the same (a quick word of warning — I don't recommend tasting everything you come across!).

This was how my love for Mother Earth developed, a love still living as strong as ever inside me. Of course, life changes; my parents passed away, my siblings married and moved on, and my best companion went to rest, all in a relatively short space of time.

For years, my love for nature was hidden, stolen by a spiritually bankrupt society, and I trod a lonely and at times desperate path. Alcohol drowned out my appreciation of life, and I didn't care. There is a whole book to be written about all this, and one day I will write it, but for now it is enough to say I met someone (in a bar of course) who persuaded me to do some writing for him, short articles for his website, and I found a new passion and reason to live. Writing was a single candle facilitating my escape from the darkness and led me back into the Light. I could be anyone I wanted to be, do anything I wanted to do, and go anyplace I wanted to go. Freedom was mine.

It was during these early days of self-rediscovery that by chance (or was it?) I met Debra and began the awaking of Nature's

Soul inside me since those heady childhood days with my four-legged buddy.

When you connect with your childhood dreams, what are the recurring clues showing up over and over in your life? What animates your senses and stirs up joyous anticipation? There are unlimited gifts inside us waiting to unfold. Imagine the endless possibilities that can and will show up as we allow ourselves to live our dreams by simply "being" in an unlimited way.

Most people give up right before their desire manifests, or they stop the rhythmic energetic frequency connecting them to what they want to do, be, or have. These 7 Concepts are meant to help you create a life of joy and infinite abundance in all areas of your life. You can do, be, or have all you desire. People do it all the time. If one can succeed, so can another.

CONCEPT #1 ON CONSCIOUS CHOICE: HOW WE CAN LEARN FROM MOTHER NATURE

Mother Nature is a great and powerful creator. She has a set of goals to help and guide her to attain her ultimate intention. She moves with one single purpose, a single purpose with many stages, from creator to re-creator with only that in Mind.

Any gardener will tell us about the wonder of planting a seed and watching nature take each tireless action she has to make to reach her purpose in the world: to flower and bear fruit before giving birth to new seeds to start the cycle again in a never-ending process. Each stage, from the production of roots and shoots to growing stems and leaves, is a powerful creative result carried out with divine intention.

We must do the same if we are to grow and bear the fruit of our labors. If not, like a diseased plant, our dreams and hopes for a better life will wilt and die — leaving us feeling physically and consciously unfulfilled.

We may be thinking nature's choices are not choices at all, merely natural happenings. After all, nature doesn't have the ability to think — does it? Well, we can use our own ability to think and consider how these natural phenomena happen. Take our master of creation, the seed, again as an example. It's in the soil, waiting for the time when the conditions are right before chemical reactions occur allowing it to send forth roots and shoots.

How does nature know the time is right? It feels it inside itself, vibrates with the Earth until their vibrations match, knows what the right frequency of vibration feels like and knows when this feeling arrives. Yet it still has to take action and trigger off its next process of growth. Nature acts and moves to its next intention or goal, to break out of its comfortable shell and produce stems and leaves, and so on and so on. If this isn't the power of decision-making by Source at its highest level, then what is! It is a thought process of some form or another still alien to many of us humans, but a natural creative process nonetheless.

The same process applies to us. We set an intention to achieve a goal, and we transmit vibrations of the intention out into the Universe. We take any physical worldly actions we can to achieve our goal, while continually vibrating our objective and waiting for the Universe to set up the right conditions. When these conditions arrive, we need to be able to recognize them, to be in tune with them. Just like the seed, we must feel them, grasp them, nurture them and grow into our intention. There we stay until the next choice to move on is made, and our intentions are transmitted to the Universe. The cycle of intention and the power of conscious choice continues until we are where we want to be.

> *"One of the most tragic things I know about human nature is that all of us tend to put off living. We are all dreaming of some magical rose garden over the horizon instead of enjoying the roses that are blooming outside our windows today."*
>
> — Dale Carnegie

A WORD OF EXPLANATION

I have various ways of connecting and working with nature in collaboration with each of the 7 Concepts. Which method I use (and it could be a combination of more than one) will depend on which concept I am working on, my local environment, the time of day and which season of the year. However, I have certain preferred methods for dealing with situations that I use whenever I possibly can, and these are what I am going to share with you at the end of each concept.

When I'm not physically among nature habitats, I love nothing better than watching nature-based films and documentaries, which I put to good use as a basis for my contemplations and meditations. By transferring my feelings and desires into images on the silver screen of my Mind and including soundtracks from my favorite musicians, I become the director and star of all the films at my own festival of life. Hold in your Mind there are no secrets to connecting with nature and your inner self; simply find the method which suits you best and use that.

STEVE'S STORYBOARD ON CONSCIOUS CHOICE

LOCATION: Nature

MAIN CHARACTER: Steve

SOUNDTRACK: Antonin Dvorak ~ New World Symphony

SUPPORTING CAST: Gardening, country walk, the elements and bird song

Getting "lost" in my own Mind-dreams playing out while I'm involved in a favorite activity is the way I discover the answers I am seeking. By this, I mean doing some gardening, going for a walk (preferably in nature), or any other activity keeping me focused on the task but allows my Mind to become clear. By immersing myself in something I love to do, I am carried away every moment I am participating in it.

I don't ask deliberate questions but allow my Mind to wander by itself, making my own personal Mind-movie and simply allowing the joy of the moment to become the director and editor in chief. I am feeling whatever I'm feeling from inside me, rather than physically thinking it. This is when the answers begin to arrive, and they arrive via a warm inner glow and bright images of each scene being played out on my Mind's movie screen, alerting me to where my inner self has taken me.

Sometimes it's a silent movie, and on other occasions a soundtrack may be included. It could be a bird, the sound of running water, or the wind in the trees. Often I am given the complete answer, but usually it is sent as a new and better perspective. Sometimes, if the moment is not right, I receive no answer at all except for an inner feeling of calm that things are working in my favor and the Universe and Mother Nature are taking care of matters until the right moment arrives.

CONCEPT #2 ON WISDOM:
THE WISDOM OF MOTHER NATURE — THE SEEDS OF LIFE

Mother Nature shows us only too well the importance of sowing seeds, but there are still many who remain blind to what is being taught, and her example is often ignored. All around us, seeds are being sown to develop into new life forms. Better and stronger species are being created in the form of new plants and trees, adapting to their environment with ever-increasing vigor.

If we misinterpret the lessons, the wisdom presented to us is lost. Nature has no secret formula. It uses methods we can all adopt and use. The biggest difference is nature doesn't give in; it nurtures its successes and doesn't worry about any failures. It simply keeps trying to do its best in every moment of every day to become the best it can regardless of the environment.

Trees and plants spread hundreds of seeds, yet perhaps only one or two will land in fertile soil and grow tall and strong. But nature, in its infinite wisdom, doesn't worry. It knows how to adapt. It is patient and waits for the right time — the right time to produce shoots, the right time to produce buds, and the right time to blossom before bearing fruit. We all already know this. Watch any gardener and he will select and sow seeds of the fruits he desires to grow into soil he has prepared. He will water and feed those seeds. He will protect them from the environment and predators. He will do all this just to achieve his desires.

If we already know this, why, oh why, will we not do the same for ourselves? Taking the time to prepare the soil of our Hearts and Souls, planting the seeds of our desires into our Minds, constantly nurturing and feeding those thoughts and protecting them from the harmful outside elements of our environment is all it takes for our lives to become fruitful.

It's time we all become wise gardeners of our own destiny, for our own sake and for the world we share. A seed will never bring us the desired results without nourishment of some kind. When our attention is on the outer world in a negative or stressful way, we should not be surprised at the results of our produce.

NURTURE YOUR DESIRES

> *"We are shaped by our thoughts; we become what we think. When the mind is pure, joy follows like a shadow that never leaves."*
>
> — Buddha

Too many beautiful ideas are aborted before they have a chance to grow. The Universe is full of them. When the idea is not accepted in surrender to the Higher Self, it moves on to another who is ready to accept and manifest it.

Let's refer to the wisdom of our great teacher, Mother Earth and her kingdoms of nature, as an example of consistency and excellence. There are about 600 families of known grasses in the world and 9,000 to 10,000 or more known species, each one coming from a single thought from Mother Nature millions of years ago. Of course this is only a fraction of all the other types of plants, shrubs, trees and vegetables she has produced.

What if nature had our present mindset and she had abandoned that single thought? Not worth thinking about, is it? In fact, if she had, we wouldn't be here right now to be able to consider it! By nurturing just one single desire at a time, we are capable of boundless abundance in every aspect of our lives. One parent thought can and will generate a whole family of love, joy, peace and harmony, not only in ourselves but in everyone and everything around us.

ON WISDOM

Mother Nature is a vibrant teacher of these wisdom principles. She manages to do so with a much more powerful voice than our own! Mother Nature would tell us we are all perfect individual human beings — musicians, artists, builders, writers, communicators, healers, gardeners or simply loving, caring parents or grandparents — each with our own special gifts from nature. As in nature as in life — we all grow, blossom, and fruit at different rates and prefer different types of conditions in which to thrive. Therefore, it should be no wonder to any of us there is no set self-development program that covers us all. What suits one may be disastrous for another. How many plants have shriveled and died in your garden purely because they were not where they were meant to be?

Each one of us has our own growing manual inside us and unless we get in touch with it we will never grow to our full potential or beauty within the garden of life. Every living thing has its own genetic code embedded within it, a blueprint of life that cannot be altered. This is why a sunflower seed grows into a sunflower, even after thousands of years of doing the same thing each and every season. Although it may develop different varieties, unique in their own way according to their local environments, it will always remain a sunflower.

As living beings, we are no different, and we should never attempt to alter the blueprint of who and what we are. Of course, we too can alter the things preventing us from growing into our full potential, but the genetic code gifted to us through our ancestors and previous incarnations is the inner wisdom guiding us on our present journey.

If we use other people's manuals, parts may work for us but only for a short time. Before long we will discover we were not completely suited to another person's soil or climate, and we begin to panic as our roots and leaves stop taking in energy. Reading books by people whose aim it is to guide us toward being able to look inside ourselves helps us to find our own growing manual. However, these people and books are only guides and the real (reel) manual should be of your own making. Be sure these people have successfully done this for themselves. If they haven't, whose story are they telling? It is only by using our personal growing manual, at our own pace, putting down roots, producing shoots, growing leaves and blossoming during the correct seasons of our lives, that we can hope to ascend to the heights of fruition.

> *"Many a man curses the rain that falls upon his head and knows not that it brings abundance to drive away the hunger."*
>
> — Saint Basil

STEVE'S STORYBOARD ON WISDOM

LOCATION: Nature

MAIN CHARACTER: Steve

SOUNDTRACK: Antonio Vivaldi ~ The Four Seasons

SUPPORTING CAST: Ancient woodlands, heath land, moors and sacred places

We have all heard at some time or another of the "Tree of Knowledge" and the "Wise Old Owl," and it is to the ancient forests and woods, and the creatures and plants dwelling among them, I go to seek wisdom. Knowledge can be learned from books and from other people, but wisdom is an inner knowing, a feeling only gained by connecting, listening, and feeling our own thoughts and emotions.

When I connect to the harmonious vibrations of nature, the pure energy the trees send out gives me sensations of calmness and humility. By raising the frequency of these vibrations, making the images in the film show of my Mind bigger and brighter, the pure and clear sounds make the whole connection a powerful and often humbling experience.

The more ancient the forest, the higher the vibrational pull I feel. Like the sap rising inside my Soul, I feel a higher sense of knowing and belief being passed into me — wisdom. These forests have been here for millions of years, long before we humans appeared. The wisdom they hold for me is so powerful, I often do not need to meditate. I simply stand and stare and see, touch and feel, listen and hear. The wisdom flows around and through me, ancient wisdom that cannot be found in schools or libraries. Nature's wisdom is out there for you, too.

CONCEPT #3 ON LOVE: MOTHER EARTH

Our Earth Mother has the option to clear everything off her surface that has not shown love toward her, as she has done many times before. It is important we clear out of ourselves that which is not loving, peaceful, and balanced: the balance of Love and Light, feminine and masculine, Heart and Mind.

Since before humankind ever appeared, Mother Nature has been changing her appearance, sometimes gradually over millions of years and sometimes violently over centuries, decades and often in an instant. At present she is in a no-nonsense mood, as we can all tell by what is happening around the globe: extreme natural and man-made disasters are occurring more frequently. We are seeing catastrophic events being played out daily on our television sets. We are fast approaching the next momentous change in Mother Nature's wondrous evolution.

Those who are not in harmony with the Universe and everything we have been gifted with by nature will be living in a less desirous frequency. Mother Earth coexists with humanity only when the love she so readily provides is returned in kind. Our ancestors, the First Nation peoples, understood this and showed respect for all living creatures, the land, the sea, the rivers and air. They took only what they needed, leaving nature able to replenish and grow.

The original meaning of the words pagan and heathen were "to be of the country; rustic" and "to live in open heath land." It was the Religious Egos of the Medieval Era that changed them into the meanings we use and think of today. Over time, these ancient pristine civilizations became corrupted by the new invading civilizations and their beliefs were considered to be undesirable and subversive. They were slaughtered or sent into slavery, their lands destroyed and their cultures distorted and twisted by the false Ego of those operating in religious zealotry with ulterior agendas of power and wealth. Since those times, humanity has rapidly lost the love and knowledge needed to co-exist, co-create, and harmonize with nature.

The literal meaning of nature is: the existing system of things; the world of matter or of matter and Mind; the creation; the Universe — in other words, "that which is born." We have traveled from a culture of "born of nature and love" into one of "made by man" and short-term feasts followed by long-term famines and drought. We have lost the loving connection with Mother Earth, and we are paying the consequences.

We live in a world of artificial Light, sounds, and smells and have lost the capability to recognize the beauty and Love nature gives us. Many children born in our man-made towns and cities have never seen the countryside, have never filled their senses, Hearts, or Minds with the joy of living, working, and playing among natural things — the things born of nature and Love as they were. The connection lays dead inside them.

There are signs more people are coming to terms with the situation and Love is returning. Many people are going back to the land to coexist and create with nature. Environmental, humanitarian, and animal welfare groups are returning Nature's

Love and healing the scars of destruction caused by the man-made world.

Each one of us has a responsibility to share the love yearning to escape from inside us and heal not only ourselves but all those connected with us — everyone and everything!

The pain we feel inside is our love crying out for freedom, and until we release it the pain will continue for eternity. The pain has caused separation of the Soul from the natural world. Only by reconnecting with our Earth Mother can we truly release this pain; only by learning the true meaning of nature and love from our ancestors and ancient civilizations will we be able to survive what is coming.

We do not believe because of the way we think. We believe because we love, and the more of us who believe and are willing to release the love we hold prisoner within us, the more powerful and healing our message will be.

> *"A flower cannot blossom without sunshine, and a man cannot live without love."*
>
> — Max Muller

STEVE'S STORYBOARD ON LOVE

LOCATION: Nature

MAIN CHARACTER: Steve

SOUNDTRACK: Vaughan Williams ~ A Pastoral Symphony

SUPPORTING CAST: Places of solitude, the wind in my face, the sound of babbling water or rain pattering through leaves

Love is a multifaceted and powerful emotion, and it can be difficult to encompass every aspect of it in our daily lives. To me, love begins with an inner feeling of self-awareness and appreciation. Love cannot be given to others if we don't have it in our own Hearts. I work at least once a day in nature to connect to and boost my own self-love with periods of deep inner peace. (This is when I use a combination of my methods and become the host of a love-based film festival.)

Finding solitude in nature clears my Mind of all thoughts apart from those of appreciation of everything I have, do, and truly am. By filling the "inner-me" spaces left from the release of negative thoughts with film clips of every positive thing that was, is, and will be in my life, my whole being eventually fills with loving vibrations.

Reinforcing my self-awareness allows me to offer my vibrations of love out into the Universe and for them to be returned to all humanity and all that is. How do I know when I have connected to my self-love? Simple, I feel at peace and wear a smile from the inside-out!

CONCEPT #4 ON PURITY: MOTHER NATURE'S PURITY

One of the best things we can do for ourselves is to place our attention upon the purity living inside us. We can learn to expand this activity through nature and her wisdom. This pure, vibrating electron can be found all around us in nature. It is vital, if humanity is to survive, to set time aside to find, or rather to rediscover, the peace and harmony within ourselves and the wonderful connection we all have with our Earthly environment — nature and Mother Earth.

There can be nothing more Soul cleansing than sitting on a cliff top and feeling the wind on our faces; listening to the roar and hiss of the huge breakers crashing against the rocks below and then receding back out into the wilderness of the ocean; hearing the cry of the gulls cart-wheeling across the sky and allowing the feeling of warmth and sense of connection with everything that is.

The peace and harmony obtained by having just a few moments of solitude is the gift of nature, the best tonic anyone can take for mental and physical healing, and it's free for us to take at any time we wish. No prescription required!

The amount of well-being that can be gained is amazing and often breathtaking, just by connecting with nature for a short time, whether it is on the cliff top, a woodland glade, the beach, or simply sitting in a peaceful garden or park.

Solitude in nature need not be — and indeed is not — a lonely place. It is the solitude of our Soul, a time of connection, a time of inner peace and healing away from the false world we have created for ourselves, a return to the womb where we were once connected to our Mother in total purity. It is a safe and comforting place to be, connected once again to the lifeblood of the feminine that is Mother Nature. We vibrate to her tune; like magnets, we attract her feelings of peace, love, and harmony with everything and everyone around us.

Nature moves and vibrates in a different time scale and frequency than we do. She knows she is eternal and is in no hurry to change, but change she does. Witness the way that, over millions of years, plants have adapted to their changing environments, forever altering their shape and form, but always with the same purity of purpose in Mind: to breathe life into the world. Witness again how the animal kingdom has evolved over thousands of years to become the creatures we know today.

Humankind has been the only creation in recent centuries to alter the environment instead of evolving with it, and today we are possibly on the brink of another cataclysm because of this. Nature has a consistent rhythm, a slow methodical beat that, over a period of time incomprehensible to us, nourishes herself for the changes she knows are necessary to live in harmony with all that is. Call it Nature's Way; call it evolution. We can call it whatever we choose. The name is inconsequential; it's the harmonious changes we need to learn from.

Only by adopting and connecting with all that is around and within us can we hope to survive as a species of nature. If we don't learn how to tune into nature's vibrations of purity, she will continue to evolve without us. Just as she has done in the past, she will rid herself of the weak and faint-hearted and nurture only the strong and willing souls who adapt, bending and swaying like trees in a storm, to grow ever stronger and self-sustainable.

> *"And this, our life, exempt from public haunt, finds tongues in trees, books in the running brooks, sermons in stones, and good in everything."*
>
> — William Shakespeare

STEVE'S STORYBOARD ON PURITY

LOCATION: Nature

MAIN CHARACTER: Steve

SOUNDTRACK: Vivaldi ~ La Tempesta di mare

SUPPORTING CAST: Waterfalls, streams, rain, rivers and oceans

Being close to water and listening to its sound or feeling its energy, like standing under the shower, hearing the rain rhythmically playing against a window pane, peacefully sitting on the ocean shore or by a gurgling bubbling stream, always brings a clarity and purity to my inner self. I suspect, at this moment, you are picturing your very own favorite watery place in your Mind's eye!

Water has the power to cleanse, bringing with it an often much-needed calmness to my Mind, Body and Soul, connecting them into a wonderful sense of unity, of being at "one" with nature and the Universe. By visualizing the impurities in both my physical and non-physical being getting washed away like edits being thrown onto the cutting room floor, and then replacing them with the healing sounds, images, and sensations of running water, leaves all aspects of me with a wonderful feeling of purity.

The beauty of this process is, once you have produced your first "cleansing movie," you can replay it time and time again, editing it to suit different situations as needed, wherever you may be. You will have your very own golden classic you'll never get tired of seeing, and I find this procedure truly empowers me to be able to function at the highest level I can in that particular moment in time.

CONCEPT #5 ON CONCENTRATED ILLUMINATION: THE CONCENTRATED ILLUMINATION OF MOTHER NATURE

Mother Nature expresses herself to us in her outward beauty, but it is beneath her surfaces she transforms herself. It is her hidden energy forming mountain ranges, pushing new land from the sea, and creating powerful currents in her vast oceans. Likewise, Mother Nature brings us beauty in her physical appearance, color and scent in the form of plants, but this too belies the true being within each and every living thing, including us.

Mankind relates to the component parts of a plant as separate entities and misses the connection between everything they truly are, because that is all we can see — the outer image. Many are blind to the being inside. A seed appears to be a seed, a root appears to be a root, a stem a stem, a fruit a fruit, and a leaf is just a leaf. Propagate any of these outwardly different-looking components and the true Soul of the plant is revealed in all its glory.

A seed does not become another seed; it grows roots and sends out shoots. A root cutting does not just turn into another root; it gives birth to new roots and sends out shoots. Likewise, stem and leaf cuttings grow into replicas of the Mother plant which lives in all of them individually and collectively.

We humans are exactly the same. Each of us has a part of our Source energy inside us, where our emotions, our guidance system, shows us the way to becoming our higher spiritual selves. At least they would be if only we learned to retune into, feel, nurture and understand their true meanings, instead of continuously listening to the conscious chatter of our Egos — our outer selves, the false world modern day society has created and which completely against our nature we battle our Hearts to comply with. If we stopped and took notice of nature and grew from the inside out, our lives would take a giant leap toward saving ourselves from self-destruction.

We need to treat our inner being as our seed of life and allow it to sprout roots and shoots which in time will grow stems upon which leaves and buds will appear, eventually blossoming into the flowers and fruits of life to share with those around us before returning to the ground as seeds. A life ends and a new one begins, all from the inside out.

If only mankind would nurture and listen to his emotions, act with his Heart, and allow his inner being to grow naturally, this world of ours would eventually be in safe hands, and Mother Earth would shine upon and within us once again.

The choice is ours. By connecting to the Love, Wisdom, and Power in our Hearts, we can take notice and enjoy being God in everything, concentrated illumination, just as Mother Nature does.

> *"I knew of course, that trees and plants had roots, stems, bark, branches and foliage that reached up toward the light. But I was coming to realize that the real magician was light itself."*
>
> — Edward Steichen

STEVE'S STORYBOARD ON CONCENTRATED ILLUMINATION

LOCATION: Universal Night Sky

MAIN CHARACTER: Steve

SOUNDTRACK: Claude Debussy~ Clair de Lune

SUPPORTING CAST: Stardust and moonlight

Whenever I am seeking a deeper or higher feeling of concentrated illumination, my favorite method is to connect with the wonder and beauty of the night sky. By simply gazing at the moon and stars I can empty my Mind by releasing all doubts, fears, and questions out into the darkness to be absorbed by the Universe and allow the ever present concentrated illumination to be returned to me ten-fold.

As in previous concepts, I find it helps to create your own imagery or Mind-film of this happening for future use, replaying it when the night sky is shrouded in cloud (and this happens a lot here in the UK!). The vastness and exquisiteness of a silent, starlit night always brings me a sensation of awe and wonder of all that is and will be in a new perspective of enlightened being.

Naturally, when this process of letting go and receiving is done in conjunction with specific phases of the moon and the alignment of other planets, it becomes an even more powerful connection with the Universal Concentrated Illumination Source energy. I suggest building your own planetarium inside your Mind. It can be built totally with your own imagination or based upon specific star and planetary movements which have special significance to you.

CONCEPT #6 ON PEACE: CHILDREN OF NATURE

> *"It is not so much for its beauty that the forest makes a claim upon men's hearts, as for that subtle something, that quality of air that emanation from old trees, that so wonderfully changes and renews a weary spirit."*
>
> — Robert Louis Stevenson

Every one of us is a child of nature. Mother Nature made us and at our death we will be reabsorbed back into her womb to be reborn time and time again. This is why, when we are connected with Mother Earth we feel at home both in nature and in our bodies, at one with ourselves and everything around us.

Have you ever wondered why we so often retreat into nature to find ourselves, to be at one with whom and what we are? The reason is: for any one of us to be able to find peace it is important to be aware of and be connected to our roots, the roots which hold us fully attuned to nature and all we belong to. Belonging to a place in nature gives us peace. It awakens us to our inner-selves. It is where we belong, and the relationship is all powerful, if only we will let it be so.

Being able to recognize this relationship is the first big step in connecting with our I AM, but to connect fully we must also learn to accept and appreciate nature for what it is: our home where we allow, accept, and appreciate the three A's of life, we will find security, love, peace and happiness in our pasts as well as our futures.

We must learn to nurture this relationship. We must respect every living thing as we would a loved family member. We must protect our environment instead of destroying it, and we should be aware when we separate ourselves from nature we destroy our relationship with it. We create our own misery here on Earth, not only for ourselves but for the whole of mankind and every other living species as well.

The relationship with your I AM Presence is no different. This is the most important relationship we will ever have. As we choose to release fear and embrace Love, we will be given tremendous assistance.

Many people have become forgetful of who they are and where their true power lives. The distractions of the "outer world" create a shadow life. These distractions are there to entice us away from our "inner world," which is our true identity/divinity leading to the freedom we each desire.

Collectively we have a choice to step out of the shadows and into the Light. We do this through purity and peace. As Mother Nature shows us, the Light feeds life. Every seed waits patiently in the darkness of the soil, gathering and nurturing the goodness surrounding it until the moment when Light warms the Earth and triggers the seed into action. Instinctively the seed breaks free of the darkness and moves into the Light, absorbing its powerful energies and transforming, stage by stage, into the perfect being.

The shadows of human ignorance and discord are fully evident. Take a look around at what has been created. Most of it is there to control us and keep us separated from our Higher Self and from each other. When we truly live in a state of peace, love, and harmony, there is nothing left to control. By reconnecting to our perfection, we're connecting to the lifeline waiting to serve us. At some point, each of us must make a choice to make changes that will bring us back to a state of peace.

Our nature, when connected to the Source of our good, is to expand, not to contract; to create, not to miscreate. We have been misusing our free will through lifetimes of ignorance and control, and we can each choose to direct the free will we have been given toward peace, love, and harmony. Peace is about harmlessness to self and others. Who can claim peace and love and then harm another? This goes against the very nature of Divine Love and Light.

So it is that all lovers of nature are appreciative of the essence of cooperation and co-creation, and it is every gardener's mantra, for without peaceful cooperation and co-creation with nature there would be no garden for him to tend and nurture; only a wilderness would exist as his landscape, and humankind itself would be lost in it.

These noble gardeners are in part the protectors of nature. They defend their plots with diligence and ruthless efficiency against outside attack — from pests and diseases, from drought and floods. They provide the right kind of soil and nutrients to produce the best fruits and blooms they possibly can. In turn, Mother Nature rewards them with her bounty, providing an abundance of food for the body, as well as for the Soul.

Observe a gardener and you will see a person who is compassionate, patient, forgiving, accepting, willing to learn and not afraid of a challenge or facing disappointment. They are at one with themselves and Mother Earth and love nothing better than to get their hands dirty in cooperation and co-creation.

As in nature, as in life: unless we nurture and protect our inner being from attack by the negativity of the outside world, we will not expand and will only contract. The world is full of dis-ease catering to all who will listen to the discord and resonate to it.

Plants can't grow in a barren land without life-giving water or nutritious food, and neither can we. Without love, compassion, joy and all the life-giving qualities of Soul nutrition, we would succumb to pain and misery. But if we learn to be the protectors of our own inner beings, the gardeners of our souls, all the things we plant in the fertile garden of our I AM will grow toward the Light again, developing into our higher selves, capable of bearing fruit and able to produce the new, healthy shoots and seeds needed for a life of calm, peace, happiness, harmony and joy. We become the masters of our own lives as nature intended us to be, living a life of eternal fulfillment.

STEVE'S STORYBOARD ON PEACE

LOCATION: Nature

MAIN CHARACTER: Steve

SOUNDTRACK: Edward Elgar ~ Nimrod

SUPPORTING CAST: Places of solitude, the wind and rain on my face, the sound of tumbling water and calling of bird song

To me, peace is an inner feeling of love for self and everyone and everything in the moment you are in. So love and peace are a marriage between my Mind, Body and Soul, and like any marriage it needs to be worked on daily if the bond is to stay strong and healthy.

As in Concept #3 (Love), I use a combination of methods to attain the peace required to face all the aspects of my life, whether they be personal, spiritual, or worldly. Finding peace by connecting with nature enables me to find the inner and outer quiet needed to bring a harmonious vibration to any situation, and by creating my own home movie I can use the visualizations at any time and in any place.

Building your own nature film archive is a way of growing and nurturing your self-love, as well as your love, empathy, and compassion toward others. Nature has overcome so many trials and setbacks across millions of years, so she is the perfect teacher, and by tuning into her energy and wisdom I receive a new and calming perspective to my life, which I call peace.

CONCEPT #7 ON RHYTHM: NATURE'S RHYTHMIC FLOW

Many of us are too afraid to make the changes we need to enable us to fully experience our true inner desires, and our own fears become compounded by the doubting words and actions of society — and even by those whom we love. Until we retune ourselves to the rhythm of life inside us as well as in everything surrounding us in nature, we will remain who we are, and what others expect us to be, until the end of our days on this beautiful planet.

The whole Universe has a rhythm we call days, weeks, months, seasons and years. We give them names, but they are truly the heartbeats giving life to everything that was, is, and will be — change! Here on Earth, Mother Nature changes with every new moment, led instinctively by her internal and external guidance systems. When we relearn to act and make changes by using our own thoughts, gut feelings, and emotions, we are becoming at one with ourselves and the Universe and can create and live the lives we, and not others, desire for us.

We see our gardens, parks, and surrounding landscapes changing throughout the year and watch the wildlife come and go, migrating and hibernating as the need to change comes over them — all done to the rhythm of life in the way it was always meant to be. It still is, so why do so many of us humans think we are any different from God's other creations and ignore the tell-tale signs showing us change is needed in one form or another?

Consider for a moment that if a tiny swift was afraid of flying the tens of thousands of miles they do each year to new breeding and feeding grounds, it would remain where it was and perish along with that bird's generations who are yet to come. This is much the same way our souls will wither if we do not let go of our doubts and fears to make the vital changes we need to survive and grow.

Consistently using these 7 Reel Concepts can awaken the sleeping God/Goddess within, fanning your Heart into a living flame of Love, Wisdom, and Power which can be expressed out into the world. Whatever we feel, we will make real in some way.

It is important to get ourselves into a place where we feel good all the time. Does it take work and effort? Yes, but like any achievement we have rhythmically practiced, such as learning to walk, tying your shoes, driving a car or learning any skill, the rewards can be great. We get to choose how we feel in every moment, and in this way the blame game is over.

If we want all that is available to us in this world, we must choose to feel good and to do whatever it takes to make it happen. This is your movie, not another's. If it is change you want, you must take responsibility. Take the appropriate steps to change the reels of your movie and you will change your life, for real.

RHYTHM CYCLES

Spending time with nature and tuning (or re-tuning) ourselves into the frequencies and rhythms of her wondrous powers of creativity, we will find balance and healing are a great cleanser of our souls. We all feel the freedom and inner peace we get by simply connecting ourselves with nature, especially when done alone, in solitude. Perhaps we are sitting under a tree or on a secluded beach, maybe even simply in our own backyard and gazing in awe at the moon and stars and allowing the sensations of the moment to wash over and into us. This is the rhythm of life we are feeling, Mother Nature's own heartbeat resonating inside us.

To understand these rhythms, we only need to look at the beating pulse of the seasons not only bringing changes to nature, they also bring changes to our own well-being: the energy of spring, the warmth and happiness of summer, the peace of autumn and the sluggishness of winter. Nature is at one with the seasons and understands how to prepare and ready her "self" for the changes she knows will come, a knowledge much of mankind has lost down the millennia.

We need to relearn these skills, to fill ourselves with these healing natural rhythms and how to stay in tune with them. Then they will be able to protect us from the "outside world"; they will help us to keep our perspective on life and stay focused on our true selves and life goals.

For those of us who have or are regaining the ability to tune into nature's rhythmic beat know that they create clarity and Light in a world of shadows caused by doubt and fear; they bring us the strength and courage to walk our chosen paths. Most importantly they bring love, a love we should cherish and share, a love we must vibrate back out into the Universe with our hopes and goals. Only in this way can our dreams be fulfilled.

Without these rhythms, there would be no Universe, no world for us to enjoy. Everything would lose its synchronicity, become unbalanced, and, well, it's not necessary to explain the outcome. This is the reason it is so important to be in harmony with the ebb and flow of nature, to feel at one and at peace with everything and everyone around us.

If you take only one thing away with you from reading this powerful book make sure that it is to create time at every available opportunity to tune yourself into the rhythm of nature. If we can all do this for only a few minutes at a time our connection will grow stronger, our desires for more understanding will expand and we will create our own gardens of self-creation.

STEVE'S STORYBOARD ON RHYTHM

LOCATION: Nature

MAIN CHARACTER: Steve

SOUNDTRACK: Richard Wagner ~ Flying Dutchman Overture

SUPPORTING CAST: Musical vibration, the sounds of nature and Her elements.

GUEST APPEARANCE: MINDFUL CREATIVITY

Rhythm is the concept flowing throughout all the other concepts, and I use the power of music as my own way of linking the methods of connecting with nature together. Music (like the Star Wars theme) is the soundtrack uniting all my Mind-movies. It gives me a buzz before the film has even started. My MP3 player is loaded with the rhythmic sounds of nature like birdsong, waterfalls, storms and even an English country garden with bees buzzing and grasshoppers chirping, so the sounds of nature are always with me even if I can't physically get out into it. The combination of using these soundtracks with the appropriate Mind-movie concept makes (in my opinion) the most powerful contemplation of them all.

When you consider every single cell in our body is resonating at its own frequency, it is no wonder certain types of music can play with our emotions, making us feel happy, sad, relaxed or agitated depending upon how in or out of harmony we are with what we are hearing. Add to all this vibrational power the images from your movies, and I think you will begin to see what I mean.

Tuning into my Mind and body helps me to feel any discord I may have, and I am able to be guided by the rhythm of my inner emotions and physical sensations to the areas of my being needing to be worked upon.

EPILOGUE: STEVE'S OUT TAKES ON EACH OF THE 7 REEL CONCEPTS

CONCEPT 1 — CONSCIOUS CHOICE

Each stage, from the production of roots and shoots to growing stems and leaves, is a powerful creative choice made and carried out with purposeful action. Choose now to be the best you can and watch the creative "you" develop and mature. It's Nature's Way, and it's your way, too.

CONCEPT 2 — WISDOM

Watch any gardener, and he will select and sow seeds of the fruits he desires into the soil he has prepared. He will water and feed those seeds. He will protect them from the environment and predators. He will do all this just to achieve his desires. All your desires grow from within. Prepare your inner self with the wisdom of nature, and those hopes and dreams will flourish and bloom.

Each of us has our own growing manual inside, and unless we get in touch with it we will never grow to our full potential or beauty within the garden of life. Every living thing has its own genetic code embedded within it, a rhythmic blueprint of life which cannot be altered. So create your own growing manual! If we use other people's manuals, parts may work for us but only for a short time. Before long we will discover we were not completely suited to another person's soil or climate.

CONCEPT 3 — LOVE

Each one of us has a responsibility to share the love yearning to escape from inside us and to heal not only ourselves but all those connected with us — everyone and everything! The pain we feel inside is our love crying out for freedom and, until we release it, the pain will continue for eternity. The pain has caused separation of the Soul from the natural world.

Plant your inner garden with Love, nurture it and share it, and reap the harvest with thankfulness.

CONCEPT 4 — PURITY

Nature moves and vibrates in a different time scale and frequency than we do. She knows she is eternal and is in no hurry to change, but change she does. Witness the way, over millions of years, plants have adapted to their changing environments, forever altering their shape and form but always with the same purity of purpose in Mind: to breathe life into the world.

Adapt and change, bend like a tree in the breeze, and grow strong and tall with the purity of nature.

CONCEPT 5 — CONCENTRATED ILLUMINATION

A seed does not become another seed; it grows roots and sends out shoots. A root cutting does not just turn into another root; it gives birth to new roots and sends out shoots. Likewise, stem and leaf cuttings grow into replicas of the Mother plant, which lives in all of them individually and collectively.

Concentrate on your wholeness; focus on being complete, and allow nature to take care of the rest...it's what she does best!

CONCEPT 6 — PEACE

Having a personal relationship with peace is the first big step in connecting with our I AM, but to connect fully we must also learn to accept and appreciate nature for what it is: our home, where we will find (if we allow, accept, and appreciate it – the 3 A's of life) security, love, peace, happiness and our pasts, as well as our futures.

Make nature your home of peace. Inwardly, mindfully, and physically live there whenever you can; it's where you belong.

CONCEPT 7 — RHYTHM

Use these 7 Concepts to create a rhythmic joyful life in tune with Mother Nature and the abundance she offers.

GLOSSARY OF TERMS

Director — The principal creative artist (you) on a movie set. A director is usually (but not always) the driving artistic source behind the filming process and communicates to actors the way he or she would like a particular scene to play.

EGO — EGO (Editing God Out)

Free Will — Freedom of choice through duality concerning free will is a controversial subject! Keep it simple for our movie. Think of our Minds, which are active and integral to free will, as being the actor making decisions in the theater of our Minds. Free will gives us the capability to "direct" the subconscious Mind, which can change our movie and therefore change our lives.

God — Our Divine Source of Love, Wisdom, and Power, which goes by whatever name we choose for personal belief comfort.

Mental Body — A receptive consciousness delivering energy, ideas, feelings, and thought patterns to our Higher Self or I AM Presence. The Mental Body evolves and transforms as we make shifts in our lives. It gives us the ability to experience contrast, discern, expand and connect with our Power, and contains many energy centers radiating Light. I think of it as a go-between us and the higher dimensions.

Higher Self or I AM Presence — Our great Perfected Presence is an extension of and connected to us. The perfection of our spirit is inseparable from us. The Higher Source of Divine Love and Light does not engage in human discord. Some describe the Higher Self as the God (Spirit) above us, living in a realm of perfection; the key to all we desire to be, to do, and to have. It is also the answer unlocking every internal door to our Souls personal journey. The name we give this presence is just as sacred and personal to each of us as is the way we communicate with this Divine Source.

Inner World — Our inner world is our private world of sacred space within, where pure consciousness lives, a place to connect with our Divine self in all its many aspects. This is a place for quiet contemplation, meditation, prayer, imagination and illumination. Our inner world, when nourished, creates a bridge to flourishing in the outer world. Looking through the lens of our inner camera into the outer world gives us endless opportunities for spiritual growth, as well as the wisdom to direct our movie brilliantly.

Movie Set — Where your movie is filmed, directed, and comes to life.

Multi-Body System — Body, Mind & Spirit

Nature Interlude — These are Steve Tallamy's synopses of each principle; wrapping Mother Nature in her infinite wisdom around each of the 7 Concepts in this book.

NOW — Naturally Occurring Wonder

Outer World — The world we live in collectively. Our individualized outer world is who we represent to the world or our outer manifestation of the influences of our inner world. The outer world can be a place of distraction for our thoughts, feelings, and actions with the ability to separate us from our inner Power if we allow it. It is also an excellent world of contrast in which to assist our inner growth and expansion. This is the bigger picture we all participate in together, and you know how hypnotic the outer world can be!

Reel Wrap — A wrap at the end of each of the 7 Concepts, finishing with a final wrap at the end of the book.

Screenplay — A script written to be produced as a movie — in this case, your movie!

Screenwriter — A person (you) who either adapts stories or writes screenplays for (your) film.

Storyboard — A sequence of pictures created (using imagination, thought, and feeling in regard to your life movie) to prepave each scene in your film production.

Treatment — A treatment is an overview of the screenplay and is used to tell the story in a concise but compelling manner.

The Critics — Criticism, judgment, gossip, blame, worries, and fear. "QUIET ON THE SET!"

Quotes — Condensed Wisdom

Universal Laws and Principles — These are Divine Laws. Energy is governed by Universal Laws and Principles. We are energy. There are many of these laws, but The Law of Love is all encompassing. Do some of your own investigation on these laws. There is abundant information available.

THAT'S ALL FOR NOW, FOLKS!

"The inner consciousness is at the background of everything and is present in everything. It is formless, and we cannot hold it, measure it, or confine it. We cannot deny its existence, because it is our very own life."

— Remez Sasson

"ROLL THE CREDITS!"

WRITTEN & DIRECTED BY
Debra Oakland

Writing a book is a life-changing experience. At least it was for me. *Change Your Movie, Change Your Life* became my teacher, friend, and confidant while seriously challenging my writing skills and typo endurance. This book is a gift of Love, which I give to myself and to you, the reader.

EXECUTIVE PRODUCER
Cody Oakland

My tireless cheerleader and husband, there are no words to describe my gratitude for your love, patience, and support. Your presence motivates and inspires me daily. You are my hero, and I love you endlessly.

PRODUCTION MANAGER
BJ Welch

Mom, you have been a source of inspiration all my life. My heart-felt thanks to you for teaching me what it means to be courageous, resilient, kind and loving.

Thank you to my sisters, Kara and Trish, and everyone who supported our family during very challenging times.

CONTRIBUTING WRITER & SOUND EDITOR/SPECIAL EFFECTS
Steve Tallamy

I love and appreciate you like a brother. Our friendship blossomed over the years, and you are family now. I have never met anyone so grounded or who loves and appreciates Mother Nature as you do. We live in different countries, yet distance is no barrier to the Heart. Thank you for accepting my request to be a contributing author. This book would not be complete without your wisdom and unconditional love of Mother Nature and her kingdoms.

COPY EDITORS

Jack Armstrong

A special thank you for your initial copy-editing skills and suggestions on this book before it went out to my editor. You are a gift beyond measure. Much love to you.

Jack is the author of *Lessons from the Source: A Spiritual Guidebook for Navigating Life's Journey*

Sigrid Macdonald

Thank you for your kindness, expertise, and discernment during the final copy editing process. I hold a heart of gratitude.

Sigrid is the author of three books including *Getting Hip, Straight and Narrow*, and *Be Your Own Editor*, and has edited more than 150 books including international best sellers *Unwavering Strength* and *Ancestor*

Gail Riena Michael

Thank you for your friendship and your support as I "wrapped" up this book!

Gail Michael is the author of *The Passions of Roxanna*

PRE & POST PRODUCTION SUPERVISOR

Kelly Lyons

Diamond Goddess, thank you for bringing such joy into my life. You will be loved and missed always. May you be held in Divine Love & Light in all your journeys beyond this earth. Your contribution in the Purity Concept on Diamonds — perfection!

FILM EDITOR

ART DIRECTOR & BOOK COVER ARTIST

Paul Bond

You were divinely sent my way. I knew who was meant to do the cover when I met you and saw your magical paintings. I am grateful for the suggestions you and your beautiful wife, Donna, made throughout the creation of this book.

Paul is the author of *The Magic Realism of Paul Bond*

SET DESIGN

INTERIOR BOOK DESIGN

Dudley & Margaux Joy DeNador

It has been my pleasure and a JOY to work with you both.Your knowledge and expertise made designing the interior of this book a smooth process. Your inner lights shine bright Dudley and Margaux. I hold you close to my heart with gratitude!

Margaux is the author of *The Art of Living a Life You Love*

CINEMATOGRAPHER
Gillian Crane

Gratitude for providing me with your view through the camera lens! Our photo shoot was picture perfect.

SUPPORTING CAST AND CREW
Deb Scott

Thank you, my Book Angel, for your ongoing assistance and encouragement.

Deb is the author of the award-winning book, *The Sky is Blue and The Grass is Green: Turning Your Upside Down World Right Side Up*

Ande Lyons

Thank you for your positive "Andelicious" support in and around this book.

Ande is the founder of *Possibility Partners*

Bobbi Hughes-Millman

The valuable assistance you provided destressed this gal and freed me up when I needed it most.

Bobbie is the author of the *Black Casket Legacy* series featuring *Darkest Frost*

Linda Doty Dunphy

Thank you for being in my life, all my life, and supporting this book with such kindness.

Heather Flaherty

There are no words to express my gratitude for your love and support. You are my sister of the Heart.

Teryl Chapel

You are a remarkable man and a valued friend. Your spiritual insight, expertise and suggestions as I was wrapping up the editing process rounded out the book beautifully. Cheers to Conscious Choice!

Judy O'Beirn

I am grateful to you Judy for all of your expert advice and assistance as this book came into reality!

Judy is the Founder & President of *Hasmark Services* and International Bestselling Creator and Co-author of the *Unwavering Strength* Book Series.

GRATITUDE FROM MY HEART TO YOURS

There are countless people who appeared on my path supplying me with invaluable friendships and assistance, encouraging me every step of the way. You know who you are! There are too many to list, but please know I am ever grateful for your love, friendship, guidance and support. This book carries the energy of Love and Light I carry for each of you in my Heart. You never know who might show up in support of just one movie-making directorial decision!

IN MEMORIAM

To my son Wade, my stillborn baby girl Reyn Tyler, my brothers Ted & Tim and my father Jim, I feel extremely blessed to have shared part of my life with each of you; and to our beloved friend Kelly. I love you all, and yes, daily miss your physical presence. I send waves of Divine Love and Light from my Heart to yours and look forward to our reunion one day.

PERMISSIONS

"Excerpt from *Don Juan DeMarco* granted courtesy of Warner Bros. Entertainment Inc."

Quotes from *The 7 Habits of Highly Effective People,* Stephen R. Covey, Free Press. Used with permission.

You Tube Video Links with permission from Andrea Gardner and Sharon Wright:

You Tube video by Andrea Gardner — The Power of Words (http://youtu.be/Hzgzim5m7oU

Your Tube video and ten-minute independent film, Change for a Dollar, written, directed, and produced by Sharon Wright at (https://www.youtube.com/watch?v=9DXL9vIUbWg

ABOUT THE AUTHOR

Debra Oakland is founder of *Living in Courage Online – A Spiritual Oasis for Overcoming Life's Biggest Challenges.* Visit DebraOakland.com to be "inspired" by over 120 of Debra's personal quotes! Debra's story and passion to teach others how to live a life in courage has been featured in major media outlets including TV, radio, magazines, and bestselling books. Debra lives in Laguna Beach, CA with her husband and best friend, Cody. *Change Your Movie, Change Your Life* is Debra's debut book.

If this book touches you in some way and allows you to live the positive, fulfilled life you were meant to live, I would love to hear from you.

Please connect with Debra Oakland on Facebook, Google+, LinkedIn and Twitter, or contact her via her website, www.DebraOakland.com.

CONTRIBUTING AUTHOR

Steve Tallamy is the contributing author of *Nature Interlude – Through the Lens of the Camera,* sharing Mother Nature's perspective on the 7 Concepts for Courageous Change. Born in Kent, the "Garden of England" in 1952, Steve developed a strong bond with Nature during his formative years. He currently lives and works in the beautiful county of Dorset on the south coast of England, sharing all that Nature has taught him whilst hopefully inspiring others to connect with Her too.

Please connect with Steve Tallamy at www.SteveTallamy.com

NOTES

NOTES

NOTES

NOTES

NOTES

30594755R00163

Made in the USA
San Bernardino, CA
17 February 2016